The Most Interesting People in Politics and History, Volume 3: 250 Anecdotes and Stories

David Bruce

Published by David Bruce, 2023.

While every precaution has been taken in the preparation of this book, the publisher assumes no responsibility for errors or omissions, or for damages resulting from the use of the information contained herein.

THE MOST INTERESTING PEOPLE IN POLITICS AND HISTORY, VOLUME 3: 250 ANECDOTES AND STORIES

First edition. September 22, 2023.

Copyright © 2023 David Bruce.

ISBN: 979-8223082989

Written by David Bruce.

Table of Contents

The Most Interesting People in Politics and History, Volume 3: 250 Anecdotes and Stories

Cover Illustration by Reuben Saturday

Chapter 1: From Activism to Death Activism

• In September 2008, James Meeks, a Baptist minister and state senator, organized an impressive act of activism. He led a boycott of Chicago Public Schools by nearly 1,000 students and instead bused them to two affluent North Shore schools. His purpose was to show the differences in funding and quality of education in the schools in different areas of Illinois. According to an article in the *Chicago Tribune*, "In a funding system fueled largely by local property taxes, New Trier Township spent nearly $17,000 per student in 2005-06 and Sunset Ridge spent about $16,000, while Chicago Public Schools spent an estimated $10,400 per pupil." A post by Paul Tough at <Slate.com> highlighted just how good New Trier Township High School[1] is, calling it "a public school with four orchestras[2], a rowing club[3], a course in 'kinetic wellness[4],' and AP (Advanced Placement) classes in French, Spanish, German, Japanese, Latin, and Chinese." The students from Chicago Public Schools were mainly black, while the students in New Trier Township High School were mainly white. Mr. Meeks said, "If they can call an emergency session for capital projects, they can call an emergency session to deal with education. This is human capital. This is a 30-year problem, the system of funding education."[1]

• In 1963, Martin Luther King, Jr. took his nonviolent movement protesting injustice to Birmingham, Alabama, in an attempt to desegregate the city. On May 2, hundreds of black children marched in the street for their rights. Unfortunately, water hoses were turned on the children, and police arrested 959 boys and girls. Nevertheless,

---

1. http://www.newtrier.k12.il.us/

2. http://org.newtrier.k12.il.us/arts/orchestras/info.htm

3. http://org.newtrier.k12.il.us/activities/NTRowing/

4. http://www.newtrier.k12.il.us/page.aspx?id=976

in the long run justice triumphed and Birmingham was desegregated. Because of such actions as this, the Rev. Dr. Martin Luther King, Jr. has been honored in many ways, including winning the Noble Peace Prize. On 20 January 1986, the United States first observed the national holiday known as Martin Luther King, Jr. Day. Also, trees have been planted in his honor in Israel, and hospitals, bridges, and libraries have been named after him. In addition, over 100 postage stamps have paid honor to him worldwide.[2]

• In 2008, voters in California passed Proposition 8, which banned gay marriage. (Because of the new law, gay couples and lesbian couples could not get married, but it was OK if a gay man married a lesbian.) Inspired by a proposition that allowed a slim majority to take away a civil right of a minority, students at Princeton University decided to attempt to pass their own Proposition 8—one that forbids freshmen from using the sidewalks. According to gay pundit Andrew Sullivan, "They don't hate freshmen—they just want to protect the sidewalks." Proponents of Proposition 8 say that freshmen are equal, but they should be kept separate. After all, allowing freshmen to walk on sidewalks is a violation of traditional sidewalk values.[3]

• Books were important in Jesse Jackson's life. While he was a child, his mother worked as a maid for a white family. She used to find books and magazines in the white family's garbage, dig them out, and take them home for young Jesse to read. As an adult, Mr. Jackson attended the University of Illinois in Urbana on a football scholarship. While at home in Greenville, South Carolina, one summer, he went to the public library to do research, but he was not allowed in the library because he was black. This angered him, and the following summer he organized a protest against the library. Television showed him and seven other students being arrested in his first protest for civil rights.[4]

• As AIDS-education activist Kate Barnhart demonstrated outside a board of education, a reporter for a Catholic TV station interviewed her. The reporter asked if she used condoms, and she answered no.

Hearing this, the reporter thought that this was a contradiction in Ms. Barnhart's position, so he asked, "You mean you don't use condoms during sex?" Ms. Barnhart explained that she doesn't have sex. The reporter then asked, "Well, since you believe in abstinence, would you recommend that other young people do as you do?" She replied, "Sure, I would recommend that all young people spend their time out here on the streets demonstrating for AIDS education."[5]

• Gay rights advocate/stand-up comedian Margaret Cho spent some time in 2009 on location in Peachtree, Georgia, where she worked out at a gym whose magazine rack was filled with magazines from Focus on the Family, an organization that would be happy if the world lacked gay sex. Ms. Cho used to bring other magazines and put them in the rack to hide the Focus on the Family magazines, but soon the Focus on the Family magazines would be visible again. So to bring visibility to the gay rights cause, she started wearing pro-gay rights T-shirts, including ones that showed two women kissing and ones that advocated gay marriage.[6]

• In the late 1980s, gay men in New York City created the organization AIDS Coalition to Unleash Power, or ACT-UP, to advocate increased AIDS research and to protest discrimination against gays. Members of ACT-UP have done such things as chain themselves to the fence surrounding the White House in an attempt to force the government to be aware of the AIDS problem and to act to solve it. The slogan of ACT-UP is "Silence Equals Death." In other words, ignoring the problem of AIDS will lead to the deaths of millions of people.[7]

• In the 1960s, African Americans engaged in sit-ins to protest segregated cafeterias and lunch counters. For example, the Georgia state legislature had a restaurant for white people only. Several African-Americans, including Ruby Doris Smith, went through the food line, selecting items of food, but the cashier refused to take their money. The Georgia Lieutenant-General came in, spoke to the African

Americans, and asked them to leave. They didn't leave, so they were arrested.[8]

• In November 1969, several Native Americans, including Dennis Banks, took over Alcatraz Island in San Francisco Bay, citing a treaty allowing the Native Americans to take possession of unoccupied federal land. Alcatraz Island was once the site of a prison but was then a deserted island. The occupation of the island lasted for nineteen months, and it succeeded in drawing attention to the problems of poverty, lack of education, and poor housing afflicting many Native Americans.[9]

• In Montgomery, Alabama, Dr. Martin Luther King, Jr., went to court to face charges stemming from his nonviolent resistance to unjust laws. The judge sentenced him to either pay a $10 fine or go to jail for 14 days. Dr. King wanted to go to jail, knowing that this action would give lots of publicity to his cause, but the segregationist authorities did not want that publicity. Someone paid his fine, although Dr. King protested.[10]

• In late 1987, Augusto Pinochet, dictator of Chile, threatened to execute 77 Chilean actors, directors, and producers if they did not leave the country by the end of November. They responded bravely by wearing T-shirts that bore the design of a red bull's-eye and the slogan "Shoot me first." The dictator backed down and did not execute the actors, directors, and producers.[11]

• Martin Luther King, Jr. was shot to death on 4 April 1968. Many people keep his memory alive each April 4 by doing two things. First, they register voters. Second, they participate in "heal-ins." Every two minutes at a heal-in, a toy gun goes pop, and people in the heal-in fall to the ground in a protest against gun violence.[12]

• French actress Catherine Deneuve is in favor of legalized abortion. In 1971, she signed an important document: the *Manifeste des 343 salopes* (the Manifesto of 343 Bitches). In this document 343 women admitted to having obtained illegal abortions. By signing the document, they hoped to change abortion laws in France.[13]

• At an AIDS die-in, some activists wore white lab coats which had bloody handprints on the backs. Others lay "dead" beside such signs as "DIED FROM RED TAPE" and "DIED DUE TO LACK OF HEALTH CARE."[14]

Advertising

• Tiger Woods signed with Nike when he turned professional in golfing. His very first Nike TV commercial featured his heritage. He is a Casiblanasian: part Caucasian, part black, part Native American, and part Asian. Unfortunately, professional golf had long been a white man's sport, although blacks could sometimes serve as caddies. In the commercial, Mr. Woods said, "There are still at least twenty-seven private clubs in this country that would not have me as a member. Isn't it time for a change?" In 1975, Lee Elders became the first African-American to play in the Masters tournament. When Mr. Woods won the Masters in April of 1997, he saw Mr. Elders. Mr. Woods hugged him and said, "Thanks for making this possible."[15]

• Before World War I, dancer Anna Pavlova saw on a London bus a huge sign bearing the legend: "ANNA PAVLOVA." The sign made her cry—she felt that advertising was fine for a can of soup, but inappropriate for a great artist.[16]

AIDS

• Many famous people have acquired the HIV virus or have died from AIDS. The first famous person to announce that he had AIDS was actor Rock Hudson, who died from the disease in 1985. In 1991, Los Angeles Lakers basketball star Earvin "Magic" Johnson announced that he was HIV-positive. Tennis star Arthur Ashe, who died from AIDS in 1993, contracted the HIV virus during open-heart surgery.

Other celebrities who have died from AIDS include Amanda Blake (who played Miss Kitty on TV's *Gunsmoke*), figure skater John Curry, pianist Liberace; Freddie Mercury (the lead singer for the rock band Queen), actor Anthony Perkins (who played Norman Bates in Alfred Hitchcock's *Psycho*), and Robert Reed (who played the father on TV's *Brady Bunch*).[17]

• One of Dini von Mueffling's best friends died of AIDS, so she became involved in educating young people about the disease. She quickly discovered that many schools wanted her to speak to students, but only if she spoke about abstinence and ignored safer sex. Once she arrived at one school that knew that she spoke about safer sex—but she was informed that she could speak only about abstinence. She declined to do so, and when she arrived at the part of her program in which she spoke about safer sex, the lights in the auditorium "mysteriously" began to flicker on and off, and she was unable to complete her program.[18]

• As figure skater Robert McCall lay dying of AIDS, he heard on the radio that he had died and he listened as the announcer read his obituary. He called the radio station and announced, "This is Robert McCall," and then he had the pleasure of using Mark Twain's immortal line: "Rumors of my death are greatly exaggerated."[19]

• Bob Rafsky suffered from AIDS, and he was an activist for AIDS research. One day, he went to a Japanese pharmaceuticals company to ask why research was being delayed on a promising new drug. To make a point, he rolled the leg of his pants up, and then showed the executives a lesion-covered leg.[20]

Alcohol

• The Rothschilds were immensely wealthy. When Paris was besieged in the Franco-Prussian War, Chancellor Otto van Bismarck stayed at the Rothschild chateau. Bismarck asked a caretaker for some wine, but the caretaker at first said there was no wine, and then later admitted that there were 100 bottles of Bordeaux on the estate. Bismarck did not believe the caretaker, so he had the estate searched, and his troops found 17,000 bottles of wine in the Rothschild cellar.[21]

• President Richard Nixon could be cheap. He once had waiters serve $6 a bottle wine to the guests at a White House dinner, even though he was served $30 a bottle wine—the waiters kept his bottle hidden in a napkin so the guests wouldn't know what President Nixon was drinking.[22]

Animals

• In 1919, the coastal steamer *Ethie* went aground off the coast of Newfoundland near Martin's Point in Bonne Bay. The crew fired rockets, which alerted people on land to the ship's plight. The people on ship needed to get a rope from the ship to land to enable people to get ashore to safety. A sailor tried to swim to shore with one end of a rope, but he drowned. Fortunately, a Newfoundland dog named Tang was on board. He was given one end of a rope, which he held in his mouth, and he swam to shore. The people on shore tied the rope securely to a stable point. The ship's crew was then able to use the rope to rig up a system of pulleys and ropes and a "beeches buoy" to allow people to reach shore. An infant was even put in a mailbag and sent to shore safely using the lifeline. Tang received credit for saving 92 lives that day, and Lloyd's of London gave him a medal for Meritorious Service, which Tang wore on his collar.[23]

• Mulla Nasruddin had two lovebirds, but he worried when they did not excrete their waste for an entire week. A veterinarian paid a house call, looked in the lovebirds' cage and asked, "Do you always line the bottom of the cage with a map of the world?" Mulla Nasruddin explained that he usually used newspaper to line the bottom of the cage, but that he hadn't been able to find any newspaper last week when he cleaned the cage and so he had used an old map of the world. The veterinarian said, "That explains it! Lovebirds are very sensitive. They haven't excreted their waste because they figure that the world has had all the crap it can stand!"[24]

• So many sightings of the ape-like creature called Bigfoot have been made around Skamamia, Washington, that the citizens passed a law making it illegal to kill a Bigfoot. Apparently, people in the state of Washington are law abiding because no one has ever been convicted of killing a Bigfoot.[25]

Art

• The artist Leonard Volk was traveling on a train going through Springfield, Illinois, when he learned that Abraham Lincoln had won the nomination for President. He visited Mr. Lincoln and asked for and was granted permission to do a plaster cast of Mr. Lincoln's face and hands. These plaster casts were later studied by Daniel Chester French, who created the sculpture of Abraham Lincoln that is seen in the Lincoln Memorial in Washington, D.C. The plaster casts reveal that Mr. Lincoln's right hand is swollen, probably from shaking so many hands as people had come by to congratulate him on his Presidential nomination. They also revealed a scar at the base of Mr. Lincoln's left thumb, the result of an accident with an axe. The scar appears in Mr. French's sculpture of Mr. Lincoln, but it is very difficult to see.[26]

• Leonardo da Vinci's *The Last Supper* is a fresco—a work of art created by painting on wet plaster. Unfortunately, this justly famous work of art started deteriorating even before he had finished painting it. In fact, fifty years after he finished the fresco, it was described as a "dazzling stain." Nevertheless, it has survived two world wars with the help of people who love it. The building housing the fresco was bombed during World War II, and all of the walls of the building were destroyed—except the wall on which the fresco was painted. Fortunately, the monks had carefully protected that wall. The fresco can be seen today at the Convent of Santa Maria delle Grazie (Refectory), Milan, Italy.[27]

• In western culture, people think of masks as things to be worn over the face—during Halloween, for example. However, in other cultures, such as in parts of Africa, a mask may also be worn on a hip, as a buckle, or over the chest. By the way, most of the wooden African masks studied by artists and scientists today are no more than 100 years old. Why? Quite simply, wooden masks don't last much more than 100 years in the tropical areas of Africa.[28]

• Among the many, many great men and women that Yousuf Karsh photographed was the gifted actress Audrey Hepburn, who was of course beautiful. Later, Mr. Karsh wanted the opportunity to photograph Chairman Leonid Brezhnev, but the Chairman would agree to sit with him, Mr. Karsh remembers, "only if I made him as beautiful as Audrey Hepburn."[29]

• American Impressionist Mary Cassatt did not want to accept prizes for her paintings, believing as she did in "no jury, no medals, no awards." Her 1902 painting *The Caress* was given a prize by the Pennsylvania Academy of the Fine Arts, but she declined to accept it.[30]

Children

• Members of the Western Mono Native American tribe still sometimes use baskets to serve as baby cradles. To protect the baby's eyes, the cradle has a hood that shades the top of the cradle. Cradles made for boys have different designs from cradles made for girls. Cradles made for boys have either straight lines or a V pattern because hunters must shoot straight to be successful. Cradles made for girls have a "busy" zigzag or diamond pattern because mothers must stay busy to take care of their families. In the old days, once the baby had outgrown its first cradle, the Western Mono used to leave the baby's cradle hanging in a young pine tree. According to tradition, this helped the baby to grow quickly like the young pine tree. Unfortunately, when non-Native American peoples moved to the Western Mono lands, they collected the baskets left hanging in the pine trees, and so the Western Mono don't follow that tradition any longer.[31]

• To combat boredom in church one Sunday, a young Sam Clemens and a friend brought cards and played a game of euchre in the vestry. Narrowly escaping getting caught, they hid the cards in the sleeves of the preacher's baptismal robes. Shortly afterward, the preacher performed a baptismal service that involved complete immersion in water, and young Sam was delighted to see three aces floating on the surface of the baptismal water. Later, Sam adopted the name Mark Twain.[32]

• Alexander the Great, who grew up to conquer much of the ancient world, was born on the same day that an important temple devoted to the Greek goddess Artemis burned down in Ephesus in Asia Minor. Later, people joked that ordinarily Artemis would have put out the fire, but she was too busy assisting at the delivery of the baby Alexander![33]

• George W. Bush was a mischievous boy. In the 4th grade, he got into trouble when he drew Elvis Presley-style sideburns on his face for a music class. The students were amused, but the teacher wasn't, so she ordered him to report to the principal's office. George was still cocky, so the principal paddled him.[34]

Computers

• Human ingenuity is astonishing. For example, computers have grown steadily smaller since their invention. In 1951, Remington Rand unveiled its new computer: the UNIVAC. It took up about 14 by 7 by 9 feet, which is the size of a small bedroom. Nevertheless, it was much smaller than previous computers, which were ten times as big as the UNIVAC! Today, an IBM, IBM-compatible, or Macintosh laptop computer can be carried around with ease.[35]

• Steve Jobs, co-founder of Apple Computer, is a computer genius, but even he has had failures. The first Graphical User Interface computer that Apple rolled out was called the Lisa, but it cost $10,000 and was reviled for being s-l-o-w. A popular joke was this: "Knock, knock." "Who's there?" Wait 15 seconds, then say, "Lisa."[36]

Death

• In the days before such things as Welfare and Social Security, people in this and other countries grew desperate because of poverty. A young mother—a struggling opera singer—who had been deserted by her husband grew desperate because her children were cold and hungry and she could not afford to give them what they needed. Therefore, she decided to kill her children and herself. She took them to a railroad track, planning to throw her children and herself in front of an oncoming train. Fortunately, her daughter, Lotta, screamed, "Mamma! Mamma! I love you, I love you! Take me home!" The young opera singer took her children home, never thought of suicide again, and after more years of struggle, became rich and famous. Her name was Ernestine Schumann-Heink.[37]

• On November 22, 1963, Jackie Kennedy wore a pink suit and matching pink pillbox hat in Dallas. President John F. Kennedy looked at her and joked, "Why is it no one cares what Lyndon [Baines Johnson, the Vice President] and I wear?" Later that day, Mrs. Kennedy stood beside Mr. Johnson as he was sworn in as President of the United States. She was still wearing the pink suit—which was now bloodstained. Jackie is buried at Arlington National Cemetery beside her husband, her stillborn daughter, and Patrick, a son who had died soon after birth. Shortly before Jackie died, she whispered, "I'll soon be with you, my little angels."[38]

• Dr. Thierry de Martel was the greatest surgeon in France at the beginning of World War II, and he was the head of the American hospital in Paris. When the Germans overran France, they removed the French wounded from the hospital and replaced them with German wounded. Then they asked Dr. Martel to continue working as a surgeon. Dr. Martel asked for a half hour to think it over, and he disappeared into his office. The Germans waited 30 minutes, then gave him another 15 minutes. When they finally walked into his office, Dr. Martel was dead—he had committed suicide rather than help the Nazi murderers.[39]

• In 1665, the Black Death, aka the bubonic plague, struck London, killing approximately 100,000 people—perhaps one-fifth of its inhabitants. Infected fleas spread the plague, although the Londoners did not know it. The Londoners attempted to stop the plague by quarantining people in their houses. People painted a red cross and the words "Lord have mercy on us" on the door of a house in quarantine. Often, everyone in a house with the plague died. Unfortunately, the quarantining did not work because flea-carrying rats were able to move freely from one house to another.[40]

• The Tlingit, Native Americans of Alaska and other parts of North America, build totem poles. The images on the totem poles recount the family history of the clan of the people who made them or the history of an important person. In the past, the totem poles often included repositories of the ashes of deceased family members who had been cremated. Unfortunately, the Christian missionaries who came to the Tlingit thought the totem poles involved the worship of the dead, so they forced the Tlingit to destroy many totem poles and to put the ashes of their dead in a cemetery.[41]

• Minor league umpire Harry "Steamboat" Johnson (1884-1951) was Jewish, but he kept that fact a secret until he was on his deathbed, when he sent for a rabbi. The rabbi was very surprised; after all, Steamboat had never attended synagogue or been involved with the Memphis, Tennessee Jewish community. Steamboat explained that he had been afraid of anti-Semitism being added to the physical abuse often suffered by the umpires of his day, and so he had kept his heritage a secret: "It's bad enough being an umpire, but to be a Jew, too, would have been terrible."[42]

• In 1769, a Franciscan priest named Junípero Serra arrived in the southern coast region of what is now the state of California. His purpose was to start missions, but many people thought that at 56 he was too old for the harsh living conditions of the California wilderness. In fact, Father Serra became so ill that some soldiers traveling with him urged him to leave California and go home again. However, the priest replied, "I shall not turn back. They can bury me wherever they wish." He recovered, and he founded nine missions before dying in 1784.[43]

• A friend of world-famous Barney's window-dresser Simon Doonan died of AIDS. Mundo was proud of his Tarahumara Indian heritage. As he lay dying, he looked at what seemed to Simon to be nothing, then said, "There are crowds of people waiting for me. They are Indians. They are weaving a banner." Simon asked, "What kind of banner?" Mundo replied, "It's a welcome banner. As soon as the banner is finished, I am going to join them." Soon, he slipped into a coma and died.[44]

• When Cesar Chavez decided to set up a union for farm workers, money was tight. He and others recruited members for the union, but occasionally it got expensive. In one case, Manuel Chavez, Cesar's cousin, recruited a new union member and collected $3.50 in union dues. Three days later, he called the union office and discovered that they already knew about the new member. The new member's wife had died, and the union had had to pay him $500 because of its death benefit.[45]

• When Mahatma Gandhi was assassinated on 30 January 1948, his last words were "Hey Rama!"—a phrase that means, "O God." Among his few possessions at his death were two pairs of sandals, a pocket watch, eyeglasses, and a bowl and a plate. By the way, when Rabbi Israel Salanter died on 2 February 1883, he also left little behind to his descendants: a pair of tefillin, a worn-out Talith, and some personal items. Rabbi Salanter is known as the father of the Musar movement in Orthodox Judaism.[46]

• John Wilkes Booth shot President Abraham Lincoln on Friday, 14 April 1865. Although physicians tried all night to save the President's life, he died at 7:22 a.m. After President Lincoln died, Secretary of War Edwin Stanton stated, "Now he belongs to the ages." When President Lincoln's son Tad learned of the assassination, he shouted, "They killed my pa! They killed my pa!"[47]

• In one of the saddest ironic moments of the 20th century, on November 22, 1963, while riding in a motorcade in Dallas, Mrs. John Connally, wife of the Texas governor, turned and spoke to President and Mrs. John F. Kennedy, who were riding in the back seat. Mrs. Connally said, "You can't say Dallas wasn't friendly." At that moment, President Kennedy was assassinated.[48]

• On Friday, 20 July 1923, Pancho Villa and four of his bodyguards were assassinated while they were riding in Mr. Villa's Dodge sedan. A street vendor shouted, "Viva Villa!" This was a signal for the assassins to start shooting. Mr. Villa died with seven bullets in his body. In 1926, his grave was opened and his head was stolen. The head was never recovered.[49]

• Italian Renaissance painter Sofonisba Anguissola is known for painting people in happy moods, although the style of the time was to paint only people in somber moods. She lived a long life, dying at age 93. In fact, she lived so long that she was forced to get a certificate of *fides vitae* to prove that she was still alive so that she could collect her pension.[50]

• After his wife died in the 1918 influenza epidemic, Italian baritone Giuseppe De Luca had built in Rome for her body a white mausoleum that included room for himself after he died. On his deathbed, concerning this mausoleum he spoke some of his last words to his doctor: "I think you send me to my little white house in Rome."[51]

• When a friend of Fred Rogers, aka Mister Rogers, was dying, she asked him, "Do you ever pray for people, Fred?" Of course, he does, and he said a prayer right then and there: "Dear God, encircle us with Thy love wherever we may be." His friend, Helen Ross, then said, "That's what it is, isn't it?—it's love. That's what it's all about."[52]

• Plague hit Milan, Italy, hard during the summer of 1484. So many people died that the living had to pile up corpses in the town square until they could dispose of them. Artist Leonardo da Vinci, who was 32 years old, was present, and he invented a perfume in an attempt to cover up the stench of the decaying corpses.[53]

• When Abraham Lincoln was a child, his mother died of "milk sickness"—an illness caused by drinking the milk of cows that had eaten poisonous plants. Before dying, Mrs. Lincoln called Abraham and Sarah, his sister, to her and told them that they should be both kind and good.[54]

• The Roman emperor Nero thought that he was a fine singer, but members of his audience disagreed. According to the Roman historian Suetonius, during Nero's recitals, some members of the audience would pretend to die so that their friends could carry them away from the recital.[55]

• Artist Marc Chagall took the death of his first wife, Bella, hard. He wrote, "A loud clap of thunder and a burst of rain broke out at six o'clock in the evening on the 2nd of September, 1944, when Bella left this world. Everything went dark before my eyes."[56]

• In the old days, a woman went into a store in Lebanon, PA, to buy a pair of men's underwear. The salesclerk asked, "How do you want them to button? Front or side?" The woman replied, "It doesn't matter. These are for a corpse."[57]

• Little Joe Monoghan (1850-1904), an Idaho prospecting and cattle businessman who stood only five feet tall, was an Old West personality with a fast draw and a secret: The undertaker discovered that Little Joe was biologically a woman.[58]

Chapter 2: From Doctors to Gifts

Doctors

• When Maria Montessori decided to become a medical doctor in Italy in the late 19th century, it was unusual for a woman to try to achieve such a career. Ms. Montessori talked to Dr. Guido Baccelli, head of the medical faculty at the University of Rome, to ask his advice. He listened to her, then told her that no medical school would ever accept a woman as a student. She replied, "I *know* I shall become a doctor of medicine." Ms. Montessori took pre-medical classes at the University of Rome, and she became the University of Rome's first female medical student. Despite Dr. Baccelli's nay-saying, on 10 July 1886, she became Italy's first doctor who was also a woman. When she was a child, Ms. Montessori was very studious. She once took a book to the theater so she could read it as the actors performed on stage.[59]

• In 1968, Pop artist Andy Warhol was shot by Valerie Solanas of SCUM (the Society for Cutting Up Men). An ambulance took him to the Columbus Hospital—Cabrini Medical Center emergency room, where doctors thought his case hopeless and pronounced him dead. Fortunately, art critic Mario Amaya, who was grazed by a bullet shot by Ms. Solanas, told the doctors, "It's Andy Warhol. He's famous. And he's rich—do something!" The doctors saved Mr. Warhol's life by opening his chest and massaging his heart, and he lived for an additional 19 years.[60]

Education

• In the 1950s, Myrna Carter attended elementary school at a segregated school in Birmingham, Alabama. During a World Series, her teacher, Mrs. Maggie Hrowbuski asked the students whom they were rooting for to win. The entire class answered, "The Dodgers!

The Dodgers!" Mrs. Hrowbuski then asked why they were rooting for the Dodgers. They didn't know, other than because their parents were rooting for the Dodgers. Mrs. Hrowbuski then taught the class about Jackie Robinson, and about the Dodgers being the first major-league team in the 20th century to allow a black athlete to be a member of the team. Myrna remembers that after the lecture, "Well, then, we knew why we were rooting for the Dodgers."[61]

• In Charlotte, North Carolina, feelings ran high when the schools desegregated. Parents worried about their children, but desegregation proceeded smoothly after Judge James B. McMillan ordered that children be bused to integrate the schools. Actually, the children themselves eased the fears of the parents. The children of black parents came home from school happy, and the children of white parents ate their breakfasts early because they wanted to be at school on time. Two white parents learned that their child had made a new friend at school, but not until the school year was half over did they learn that their child's friend was black.[62]

• Becoming pregnant as a teenager can affect one's life in ways one can't imagine ahead of time. For example, Kerry was claustrophobic—afraid to be in small, enclosed spaces such as elevators. After becoming pregnant at age 17, she kept attending school for a while—but eventually her pregnancy became so advanced that she no longer could climb the five flights of stairs at school. Because of her claustrophobia, she couldn't take the elevator, so she quit school. (Fortunately, after giving birth, Kerry began attending an alternative school—one designed for students such as herself who had fallen behind in schoolwork.)[63]

• Amelia Earhart was not especially popular in high school. She wrote, "I don't think that boys especially cared for me, but I can't remember being very sad about the situation." In her 1915 high school yearbook, the caption under her name reads, "The girl in brown who walks alone." She did not bother attending graduation and didn't pick up her diploma. However, in 1932, the mayor of Chicago presented it to her at a public reception honoring her.[64]

• People today are worried about school shootings, and that has led to conformity at high schools today. Michael Moore, director of *Roger and Me*, visited a school, and the students told him that they all wore white or some neutral color because anyone who wore black or something original was asking for an invitation to visit the principal, who would want to know if the non-conforming, original student was thinking of shooting up the place.[65]

• While attending law school in Tuscaloosa, Harper Lee, the author of *To Kill a Mockingbird*, ran into a professor who attempted to get the female law students to describe the lurid details of such crimes as rapes. The female students did not put up with this. One female student who declined to be manipulated into describing lurid details told him, "Look, you know about the male anatomy—why don't you just tell us?" The students in class applauded her.[66]

• Some very successful people have been poor students. Paul Orfalea, who founded the Kinko's chain, got D's in school and got thrown out of four schools. He also failed a couple of grades, and when he finally graduated from high school, he did so at the bottom of his class. He recalls, "In third grade, the only word I could read was 'the.' I used to keep track of where the group was reading by following from one 'the' to the next."[67]

• President Woodrow Wilson's golf game was interrupted once at the Brannockburn golf course when someone grabbed his caddy by the ear and started to take him away. It turned out that the caddy was a hooky-playing schoolboy named Al Houghton and the man pulling the caddy off the course was his teacher. President Wilson convinced the teacher to allow young Al to finish the round and then return to school.[68]

• The parents of Marian Wright Edelman were serious about raising their children correctly. If one of their children wasn't busy, they would assign the child a chore to do. However, if the child was reading, they would let the child read. Ms. Edelman says that she and her siblings read a lot. In 1973, Ms. Edelman founded the Children's Defense Fund, which lobbies politicians to pass legislation to help children.[69]

• The Native Americans known as the Western Mono are basket makers. One of their traditions is that a basket maker must give away the first basket that she creates—this encourages generosity. Contemporary basket makers such as 11-year-old Carly Tex learn the craft by making baby cradles for dolls.[70]

• A politician asked a Zen master, "Your Reverence, what is egotism?" The Zen master replied, "If you don't understand that, you must be an idiot." The politician's face became red with anger, and the Zen master said, "Your Excellency, that's egotism."[71]

• In 1942, Robert Trias, the United States Navy's middleweight boxing champion, got into the ring with a kung fu master and discovered that the kung fu master was so quick that he couldn't hit him. After the "fight," Mr. Trias began to study kung fu.[72]

Elections

• In 1868, Ulysses S. Grant won a close race for United States President. His margin of victory in the popular vote was only 300,000, and the voters who put him in office seem to have been 500,000 recently freed slaves. Following the Civil War, former slaves were given the right to vote and federal troops made sure that they were not prevented from voting. Only later did the South begin a concerted effort to keep African Americans from voting.[73]

• When Howard J. Baker, Jr., the U.S. Senator from Tennessee, decided to run for President, he told his feisty grandmother, who responded, "Look, Howard, I'm going to support you. But I'll tell you right now if you really want to go where the power is, run for Sheriff."[74]

• While they were standing in line to vote, a friend told author Michael Thomas Ford, "I always vote for the one who tells the best lies."[75]

Evil

• Canadian figure skater Toller Cranston once served as a judge at a Miss USA beauty pageant, where he became aware of the often-unnoticed oppression of women—even women who seem privileged. Because the current news included such stories as the rape trials of Mike Tyson and William Kennedy Smith, and the allegations of sexual harassment against Clarence Thomas, when it was his turn to interview the contestants, Mr. Cranston asked, "If you had been the judge, how would you have sentenced Mike Tyson?" To his surprise, the first contestant he asked this question broke down and told him that she had been raped. In all, three of the contestants had complete breakdowns when asked the question and several were unnerved by the question. Afterward, Mr. Cranston estimated that 10 of the 50 contestants had been raped.[76]

• When the *Titanic* was sinking on 15 April 1912, Fourth Officer Joseph Boxhall saw a ship only four or five miles away. He attempted to use a Morse code lamp to signal the ship that the *Titanic* was in distress and needed aid, but the ship sailed away. In addition, the crew of the *Titanic* was shooting distress rockets into the air and using the wireless radio to send a CQD signal. (CQD was a forerunner of the SOS signal and meant "Come. Quick. Danger.") Later, an investigation revealed that the *Californian*, a ship piloted by Captain Stanley Lord, had seen the distress rockets set off by the *Titanic*, but had done nothing about them. Captain Lord didn't even have his men turn on the wireless radio to check for a distress signal.[77]

• On 1 December 1854, a national referendum was held in Mexico to determine whether Antonio López de Santa Anna should continue in office as President of Mexico. Voters signed their names in one of two books: one book recorded votes favorable to Santa Anna, and the other recorded votes against Santa Anna. After the referendum, in which the citizens of Mexico overwhelming voted that he continue in office, Santa Anna arrested everyone who had signed the book that recorded votes against him.[78]

Fathers

• Back when actor Paul Newman was campaigning for Eugene McCarthy, he attracted many people to hear his speeches—not just voters, but also young admirers. At a speech at an American Motors plant, he stated, "I just want to make one thing clear. I'm not here because I'm an actor. I'm here because I got six kids, and I'm worried about their future." At this point, an infatuated young brown-haired girl called out, "Oh, Paul. Adopt me."[79]

• Barbara Bush, the wife of one President and the mother of another President, called her parents Daddy and Mommy until she got married. Her father did not care for anything fake. Once Barbara went on a date with a boy and said, "Good night, Father." Daddy answered, "Good night, Bobsy. Keep your nose clean." (By the way, she hated the nickname "Bobsy.")[80]

• When the armistice was declared in World War II, investigative reporter I.F. Stone's father wanted to ring the bell at the local fire station; however, he was informed that he would be fined $5 for ringing a false alarm. His father was in such a celebratory mood that he rang the bell and paid the $5.[81]

Food

• Establishing missions in the New World was a tough job. In 1769, Father Junípero Serra founded the first mission in Alta California (now the state of California). The mission was called San Diego de Alcalá, and soldiers protected it. Unfortunately, times were rough, food grew scarce, and the soldiers even ate their mules for food. Captain Gaspar de Portolá had requested that a supply ship bring the mission food, but the supply ship was slow in coming. Finally, Captain Portolá ordered the missionaries to abandon the mission if the supply ship had not arrived by 19 March 1770. On that date, the missionaries and soldiers saw the ship, but it continued to sail northward. Captain Portolá again wanted the missionaries to abandon the mission, but Father Serra argued that the ship was a sign that they ought to stay. In a few days, the ship, loaded with food and supplies, sailed into the San Diego harbor, saving the mission.[82]

• According to ancient stories, the Native American tribe of the Ojibway (also known as Chippewa) once resided by the Atlantic Ocean; however, prophets told them that they must move west to find a better land on which to live. They would know that they had found the right land when abundant food grew in the water. The Ojibway migrated west for hundreds of years, and in the mid-1500s, they came to what is now northern Minnesota and Wisconsin. There they found wild rice growing abundantly in the water. The wild rice, called by the Ojibway *mahnomin*, is a gift from the Creator and is their sacred food.[83]

• In the early days of the Foxboro company, a technological advance was desperately needed. Fortunately, a Foxboro scientist walked into the office of the company president with a working model of the needed technological advance. The company president was overjoyed and wanted to give a present to the scientist right away to show his appreciation, so he grabbed the first thing that was handy—part of his lunch—and thrust it at the scientist, saying, "Here—have a banana." Today, to recognize employees who demonstrate creativity and innovation, Foxboro gives the high honor known as the Gold Banana (a lapel pin).[84]

• Very early in his career, Russian bass Feodor Chaliapine came at times very close to starving. Often, he slept long hours, because when one is asleep, one is not hungry. He writes in his autobiography, *Pages From My Life*, that sometimes he slept for "more than forty-eight hours at a time." (He discovered that it was possible to get used to being hungry for two days in a row, but unfortunately sometimes he had no food for three or even four days in a row.) By the way, Spanish painter Francisco Goya painted very few still-lifes during his career. His still-lifes of food were painted in Madrid in 1811 at a time of warfare when food was scarce. Apparently, he painted from memory due to the lack of food.[85]

• Corn was an important crop for the Winnebago, Native Americans are also known as Hochunk. The Winnebago knew how to take care of the corn and of the land on which they grew the corn. They would plant corn in a different area each year, thus allowing the land they had planted the previous year to lie fallow and refresh itself. In addition, when planting the corn, they would often bury small dead fish along with the corn seeds in order to fertilize the soil. By the way, if you want to say a prayer in the Winnebago (Native American) language, just say *Myoona* (Great Spirit) *Peenagee-gee* (Thank you). When you're hungry, this prayer has the advantage of being only two words long.[86]

• The young Martin Luther King, Jr., got a taste of freedom from prejudice while picking tobacco for cigars during a summer job in Hartford, Connecticut, because no Jim Crow laws existed there. However, during his train ride back home to Atlanta, Georgia, he experienced a change in laws. Up North, he could eat in the dining car with white passengers, and no one minded. However, once the train reached Virginia, he had to eat in the rear of the dining car behind a curtain so no white person could see him.[87]

• One of the most unusual meals ever eaten by human beings was over 2 million old on 13 January 1951, at the 47th Explorers Club Annual Dinner. Arnold Haverlee was an explorer, a scientist, and an amateur chef. He was also a member of the Explorer's Club and planned its annual banquet. Once, he heard about a mammoth that had been frozen under the Juneau ice cap for over 2 million years, so he arranged to have it delivered to New York, where he cut steaks out of it.[88]

• In a religious vision, Muhammad, the prophet of Islam, met other prophets, including Abraham, Moses, and Jesus. Offered his choice of water, milk, or wine to drink, Mohammed chose milk. This represents a middle way between the asceticism of drinking water and the epicureanism of drinking wine. Thus, Islam avoids being too strict and avoids being too easy.[89]

• The Tlingit, Native Americans of Alaska and other parts of North America, smoke salmon during the summer months. This can be hazardous. No, the salmon aren't dangerous, but bears like to break into smokehouses and steal the salmon. Sometimes, the Tlingit complain that bears are too lazy to catch fish for themselves.[90]

Free Speech

• On a video blog, famous atheist Penn Gillette of Penn and Teller fame made an argument that people ought to proselytize. If you're a Christian, let people know why you are a Christian. If you're an atheist, let people know why you are an atheist. Basically, a marketplace of ideas exists, and if you have people giving arguments for what they believe, the best arguments will—all of us hope—win. Of course, Penn thinks that arguments for atheism are the best arguments and therefore the arguments that will win. One bad thing that happened is that many Christians did not respect his intellectual property. They burned his video blog to DVDs without his permission and showed it in churches and preached sermons about it. One good thing that happened is that most or all of the churches respected his ideas. Some of the profanity may have been bleeped out, but Penn's arguments for atheism remained intact. One very good thing that happened is that Campus Crusade for Christ wrote him a nice letter and asked him for permission to use his video blog. He said yes to their request. In his book *God, No!*, Penn wrote, "They were playing by the rules, and I like that."[91]

• Jane Addams of Hull House (a settlement house for newly arrived European immigrants in Chicago, Illinois) was truly independent. She spoke her mind against millionaires, and when working-class people worried that she would stop speaking her mind once she was subsidized by millionaires, she replied that she intended never to be subsidized by millionaires nor to be bullied by the working class and therefore she would say whatever she wanted without consulting either group. In 1931, Ms. Addams became USAmerica's first woman to win the Nobel Peace Prize.[92]

• Musician Bob Dylan declined to be censored. Once, he was scheduled to appear on *The Ed Sullivan Show*, but during rehearsal, the producers tried to tell him that he couldn't play certain songs on the television show. Mr. Dylan picked up his guitar and left. Someone else took his place on the show.[93]

• When the album *Jesus Christ Superstar* by Tim Rice and Andrew Lloyd Webber came out, the rock opera was controversial and sometimes even banned. Arkansas' biggest radio station banned the single "Superstar." It also banned all records produced by the record's label: Decca.[94]

• Dictators, of course, don't like to be ridiculed; that's why the following proverb was prevalent in World War II Germany: "Silence is golden, speech is Dachau."[95]

Gays and Lesbians

• In 2008, at Ponce de Leon High School in Holmes County, Florida, some students taunted a senior because she was a lesbian. She asked a teacher's aide for help, the teacher's aide informed principal David Davis, and Mr. Davis told the student that it was wrong to be gay, and he informed her parents that their daughter was a lesbian—her father wanted to kick her out. Other students wanted to show support for the lesbian student, so they started wearing gay-friendly T-shirts and started writing "Gay Pride" on their bodies. The principal responded by banning these forms of free speech. A brave heterosexual student, Heather Gillman, who has a lesbian cousin, responded by writing the school board, which backed up the principal's ban on free speech. She then sued the school board. Federal Judge Richard Smoak, a Republican appointee, came to the rescue, and in the 2008 court case *Gillman vs. School Board for Holmes County*, he stated, "The robust exchange of political ideas is essential in a vibrant, progressive society and is precisely the type of speech that is sacrosanct under the First Amendment." The ban on free speech was lifted at Ponce de Leon High School in Holmes County, Florida. In fact, the judge ruled, "Defendants are ordered to take such affirmative steps necessary to remediate the past restraints of the expression of the support for respect, equal treatment and acceptance of homosexuals, including but not limited to notifying in writing the Ponce de Leon High School student body and the middle school students and school officials within Holmes County school district that students are permitted to express support for, respect, equal treatment and fair acceptance of homosexuals...."[96]

• Back in the 1950s, police officers used to entrap homosexuals. Police officers would pretend to be gay, hoping that a gay man would flirt with them. If a gay man did flirt with them, the police officers would arrest the gay man. Most gay men were afraid of being outed, so they would not resist the charges. In June 1952, a gay man named Dale Jennings did resist the charges in court. His lawyer showed at one point that the police officer was lying, the jury could not reach a verdict, and the charges were dismissed. Mr. Jennings, a true American hero, was the first gay man not to let himself be intimidated by police officers. By the way, psychiatrists used to think that homosexuality was a mental disease that could be cured by such treatments as electric shock therapy, internment in mental hospitals—and lobotomies.[97]

• All his life, Kevin Berrill felt different from other people, and when he reached adolescence, he discovered that he was gay—he had sexual feelings for other males. Unfortunately, because of what his society believed at the time, he thought being gay was bad and he resolved to stop being gay—or, if he failed to stop being gay, to hang himself when he became 17 years old. Fortunately, however, he acquired information about gay people, and even more important, he met other gay people, and so he did not kill himself when he reached his seventeenth birthday. Instead, he became a happy gay adult.[98]

• Not all parents react well when learning that one of their children is gay. A daughter once told her mother that she was a lesbian, and her mother told her, "I thought you were going to tell me you were a heroin addict, and I wish you were, because that I could fix. I can't fix this, and I wish you were dead." Today, the mother regrets her words.[99]

• The first political party platform to include a gay rights plank was the Democratic party platform of 1980, when Jimmy Carter and Walter Mondale were running for President and Vice President. The party platform also included support for the rights of African-Americans, Native Americans, Hispanics, and Americans who live abroad.[100]

Gifts

• In September of 1993, Colin Powell, a four-star general, formally retired as a United States Army officer. President Clinton presented the Medal of Freedom to General Powell, and he gave him the retirement gift that General Powell's friends had specially picked for him: a rusty 1966 Volvo. No, the rusted-out auto was not a joke. General Powell's friends knew that he enjoyed working on old Volvos and turning them into something that could be a source of pride to own—and to drive. The gift was much appreciated.[101]

• After Anna Pavlova had danced her last performance in Sydney, Australia, a young girl presented her with a boomerang, then said, "The boomerang comes back, and we hope you'll come back, too."[102]

Chapter 3: From Good Deeds to Mothers Good Deeds

• At age 12, a girl named Ray Kaner entered Auschwitz. Five years later, her growth was stunted, she was very thin, and she looked like a very young child. The Nazis moved her to Hambieren, Germany, to do heavy labor. Fortunately, Willy Minke, a 60-year-old guard, took pity on her and smuggled food to her to keep her alive. He also was able to find her a different, easier job, working in the German officers' barracks. Ray survived the Holocaust, but she spent months in a hospital, separated from Mr. Minke. After finally recovering, she searched for Mr. Minke, and discovered that the Allies had arrested him after the defeat of the Nazis. Fortunately, he had helped many other Jews who had testified for him and had gotten him released. Until he died, Mr. Minke and Ms. Kaner were friends.[103]

• Although his own home was unharmed, Rabbi Chaim slept in an emergency shelter after a fire had swept through Brisk, leaving many people homeless. Rabbi Chaim explained his actions by saying he could not sleep in his own home while so many were homeless. Besides, if he slept in his own home, the fundraising for building homes for the homeless would take a long time. But if everyone knew that their Rabbi was sleeping in an emergency shelter until the new homes had been built, the fundraising would go much faster. Rabbi Chaim slept in the emergency shelter until the new homes were built.[104]

• During the American Civil War, the Union ship *Commodore* was used as a floating hospital. On one occasion, a gunboat manned by Confederate sailors sighted it. The *Commodore* was in danger of being fired on, but the nuns who served as nurses stood against the rail nearest the Confederate gunboat. The Confederate sailors saw the nuns' habits, realized that the *Commodore* was being used as a floating hospital, and did not fire on it; instead, they let it continue its journey.[105]

Hoaxes

• The Bible contains stories of giants such as Goliath, so many people believe that giants once walked the earth. In the mid-1800s, a man named George Hull decided to help that belief along. He and a business partner, H.B. Martin, hired a couple of sculptors to make a "giant corpse" from a 5-ton block of gypsum, then Mr. Hull used a darning needle to make hundreds of holes resembling pores in the gypsum. He then buried the "corpse" in a farm located in Cardiff, New York, and a year later he hired two workers to dig a well where the "corpse" was buried. Of course, they unearthed the "corpse," and of course Mr. Hull made money exhibiting it. Even after Mr. Hull admitted that it was a fake, people still came to look at it. Even today, people come to look at the fake. In Cooperstown, New York, a popular exhibit of the New York State Historical Association is the "Cardiff Giant."[106]

• In January of 1993, media reported that on Super Bowl Sunday violence against women increased and as many as 40 percent more women would be battered that day than on any other day. However, this turned out to be a hoax. Researchers who had actually studied violence against women had NOT discovered that violence against women increased on Super Bowl Sunday.[107]

Holocaust

• Many of the non-Jewish people who rescued Jews during World War II emigrated later to Israel, where they were ignored and mistreated. For example, Stefan Raczynski saved many Jews in Poland by feeding them and giving them a place to stay when they came out of the forest. After Stefan moved to Israel, his son wanted to become a pilot for the Israeli army, but they told him, "Your father is a Polish Catholic; you won't be a pilot." Stefan then went down to talk to them, and his son became a courageous pilot. On another occasion, some religious Jews threw stones at his house and screamed, "Go away, goy." (Fortunately, not all Jews were like that, and late in the lives of the rescuers, Israel began to give them a pension in honor of their services to Jews during World War II.)[108]

• Jonka Kowalyk and her widowed mother hid Jews during the Holocaust. This was dangerous, as the Nazis executed people who were found hiding Jews. Occasionally, the Nazis almost found the Jews whom Jonka and her mother were hiding. Once, the Nazis entered an attic that the Jews had just left. Playing cards were out in the open, as were some cigarette butts. Jonka's seven-year-old nephew had followed the Nazis upstairs while the women remained downstairs, and he whispered to the Nazis, "Don't tell my mother. She'll kill me." He managed to convince the Nazis that he and his friends used the attic to smoke and play cards in. The Nazis stopped hunting for Jews that day.[109]

• Branko Lustig used his wits to stay alive in the Holocaust. He worked in the Birkenau coal mines, but caught typhoid fever and was put on a truck going to the crematoria, where he knew that he would be exterminated. He jumped from the truck, and on the road he saw a group of running naked prisoners whom guards were herding to Auschwitz. Mr. Lustig stripped off his clothes, and he managed to join the group of running naked prisoners. At Auschwitz, he and the other prisoners were tattooed, but at least he was still alive. Following the Holocaust, he studied film and television, and he became a co-producer of the movie *Schindler's List*, which was directed by Stephen Spielberg.[110]

• During World War II, Antonín Kalina helped rescue 1,300 children in Buchenwald by putting them in his block and by putting up a sign saying "Typhus" so that no German would come near them. He also told the Jewish children (1,200 of the 1,300 children were Jewish) to say they weren't Jewish if they were asked—or he would hit them.

In addition, he tried to keep the children amused, but soon discovered that laughing and playing were impossible for them—they had seen their parents die.[111]

Hunting

• When young adult author Chris Crutcher was growing up in a small town in Idaho during the 1950s and 1960s, students who won varsity letters also joined the C Club, which used to raffle off a shotgun every year. Students bought tickets for the raffle, and whoever won the raffle was given the shotgun at school during school hours. In addition, the high school parking lot usually had a few pickups with a gun in the gun rack during hunting season.[112]

• John Piche is a member of the Native American tribe known as the Cree and works as a guide near Fort Chipewyan in Alberta, Canada. He both hunts and fishes, but he believes in eating what he kills, so he works as a guide only for people who believe as he believes. He is against sport hunting, so he declines to work as a guide for sport hunters.[113]

Illnesses and Injuries

• Competence is extremely important in life. In Sudan, relief worker Julie Mayotte wanted to watch the dropping of 31 tons of food from an aircraft. The food would be dropped in 100-kilo sacks. (One kilo is approximately 2.2 pounds.) Problems have occurred during these food drops. When the United States dropped food for thousands of starving Kurds, the Kurds rushed to the falling food, and many Kurds were crushed to death. Ms. Mayotte was watching at a safe distance from the drop site, which was clearly marked by two targets. The food was supposed to be dropped between the two targets. Unfortunately, something went wrong. The food was dropped directly over Ms. Mayotte. Hundreds of heavy bags fell, and one hit her. She called her,

"I'm hurt. It's my leg. It's really bad. The bones are sticking out all over." Only half of the food was dropped on the first pass. The second half was supposed to be dropped immediately, but of course the second pass was cancelled due to Ms. Mayotte's injury, although she wanted the drop to continue because the food was desperately needed: "Don't let this stop the show. Please." Her lower leg was broken in 12 places, and her upper leg and hip were also injured. A surgeon told her that she had two choices: 1) Try to save the leg. This was barely possible, and it would take one or two years of reconstructive surgery, with no guarantee of success, or 2) Amputate the leg below the knee now, and let her get on with her life. Ms. Mayotte said, "Take it off. I've got a life to lead." The surgeon amputated her leg, and she continued to do good works, but the injury, pain, and amputation were all unnecessary. Somehow, the airplane pilot did not know how to correctly drop the food, and a disaster occurred.[114]

• Antonio López de Santa Anna became President of Mexico five times in the 19th century, but his ego was immense, and he seems to have been looking out for himself—with some exceptions at times—much more than for the people of Mexico. In his old age, he returned to Mexico from exile, and he was saddened that people did not recognize him. He was going blind, but when a doctor told him that he could have an operation to remove his cataracts and restore his sight, he replied, "If being blind, I suffered so many ingratitudes on returning to my homeland—what would I do if you again restored my sight? No, I do not wish to see; leave me sunk in darkness, I am more tranquil thus."[115]

• One reason the Native Americans could not mount a more effective resistance to whites who illegally took over their lands was that the whites brought highly contagious and deadly diseases such as smallpox that devastated the Native Americans, who had not developed an immunity to them. In 1763, the British acquired blankets from a hospital that treated patients who had smallpox. The British then gave the blankets to Native Americans, deliberately trying to infect them with smallpox so that many of them would die, thus decreasing their ability to resist the whites.[116]

• President Franklin Delano Roosevelt could not walk on his own, and great care was taken to hide that fact from the public. He declined to appear in public with crutches or in a wheelchair. To appear to walk on his own, he would walk while tightly holding the arm of a supporting son or friend. In addition, he would enter buildings by routes where he could not be seen. For example, once he was carried up a fire escape. On another occasion, the fire escape was too narrow for someone to carry him, so he dragged himself up the fire escape with his arms.[117]

• A man named Kid Hogan fought in World War I—the patriotic slogans for this war included "The War to End All Wars." He was badly wounded just before peace was declared, and he was eventually shipped home. When his mother picked him up, both of his legs were completely missing, one of his arms was completely missing, and part of his remaining arm was missing. Kid Hogan looked up at his mother and said, "Hello, Momma, we won."[118]

• Barbers often have red-and-white poles outside their establishments. This custom goes back to the Middle Ages, when barbers would often perform bloodlettings. (They cut people as well as cutting hair.) People at the time believed that a cure for illness was to remove blood from the ill body. The red of the barber pole represents blood, and the white of the barber pole represents bandages.[119]

• Mary Walsh served as a nurse in Vietnam, and she was present on November 11, 1993, when the Vietnam Women's Memorial was unveiled in Washington, D.C. At the ceremony, she met a former patient, a veteran in a wheelchair. The veteran smiled at her and said, "I wanted to find you." Then he stretched out his right arm and added, "To show you I can use my arm again."[120]

Language

• Judge Roy Bean, the Law West of the Pecos, also served as coroner. Once, he had to travel a hard 15 miles on mule back to investigate an accident. Falling timbers had crushed ten men, seven of whom were dead. The other three men were badly wounded. Judge Bean looked over all the men, and because he didn't want to have to make a second 15-mile trip on mule back a few days later, he ruled that all ten men had died in an accident. He explained, "Them three fellas is bound to die." Of course, as you may expect, Judge Roy Bean, aka the Law West of the Pecos, didn't know much law. Once, a lawyer referred to *habeas corpus* in Judge Bean's courtroom and the judge threatened to fine him because of his use of bad language.[121]

• Elaine L. Chao, who has been Director of the Peace Corps, Secretary of Labor, and President and CEO of the United Way, came to the United States to be with her father, who had emigrated from Taiwan three years previously. She did not know a word of English, but in the third grade she wrote down everything that the teacher wrote on the chalkboard. Her father, who worked at three jobs, would come home from work, look at her notes, and then explain the lessons to her. In that way, she learned English.[122]

• It is often useful for a Catholic priest to know more than one language. Msgr. Vincent Fecher was assigned for five years in the Philippines, where he prepared his sermons in Tagalog, then he was assigned for five years in Rome, where he prepared his sermons in Italian, and finally he spent the rest of his career in Texas, where he prepared his sermons in English (but also learned to speak Spanish and Tex-Mex).[123]

• Governor Huey Long of Louisiana (1893-1967) once said about the Imperial Wizard of the Ku Klux Klan: "... when I call him an s.o.b., I am not using profanity but am referring to the circumstances of his birth." Also, Canadian Prime Minister Pierre Trudeau was once thought to have mouthed the f-word in the House of Commons, but he claimed that the word he was mouthing was "Fuddle-duddle." By the way, an Ohio University art teacher once composed an email with as many words beginning with the letter "f" and then referred to it as her f-word email.[124]

• Black comedian Dick Gregory's autobiography is titled *Nigger* (please don't accuse me of racism—that's really the title), and his dedication is: "Dear Momma—Wherever you are, if ever you hear the word 'nigger' again, remember they are advertising my book." That's pretty good—turning a racial epithet into an advertisement for a book by a black man.[125]

Humorist Ellen Orleans writes about code words that lesbians use to identify other lesbians. For example, there's "She goes to the same church we do" and "She's family." Some lesbians even use the code words "She's a member of the committee" and "She's advanced." Others use "gay-dar" and say "Beep, beep" when they pass a lesbian.[126]

• The use of the word "cell" to describe certain structures in nature that can be seen only with a microscope was invented by the 17th-century scientist Robert Hooke. He used a microscope to look at a thin slice of cork, and he observed that the cork was divided into many, many small boxes that reminded him of the cells that monks live in.[127]

• When 19th-century political cartoonist Thomas Nast went to Guayaquil, Ecuador, after being appointed consul general by President Theodore Roosevelt, friends asked why he was going to such a "God-forsaken place." Mr. Nast joked that he was going in order to learn the correct way to pronounce its name.[128]

Media

• In 2009, the city council of Tucson, Arizona, fired city manager Mike Hein. Mr. Hein is a personal friend of *Tucson Weekly* columnist Tom Danehy, who regarded the firing as the dumb action of a smart city manager by dumb politicians and wrote forcibly about it. After he wrote about the dumb action, the smart city manager, and the dumb politicians, a woman who had read his column asked him, "Are you the horrible person who wrote those awful things about the [City Council members]?" Mr. Danehy replied, "I'm one of them." The woman then said, "How do you get away with writing things like that? You probably don't even know [City Council members] Karin Uhlich or Regina Romero. How can you call them 'dumb'?" Mr. Danehy replied, "Because the editor probably wouldn't have let me use 'f—in' ignorant.'"[129]

• Photographers can be remarkably insensitive. Shortly after Charles, Jr., the 20-month-old son of Charles and Anne Morrow Lindbergh, was kidnapped and murdered although the Lindberghs had paid the $50,000 ransom demanded for his safe return, a speeding car forced a car carrying their other son, Jon, to the side of the road, and men jumped out and took photographs of the crying child. The photos appeared in a newspaper the following day.[130]

• More and more presidential candidates have taken illegal drugs. During an interview broadcast on CNN, Bill Bradley, who ran for President in 2000, was asked if he had ever tried marijuana. He replied, "On several occasions." He was then asked if he had inhaled, and he replied, "I did indeed."[131]

• When you ask horror writer Stephen King what he reads that scares him, he answers, "*The New York Times.*" This answer makes sense. What is more horrifying than war, crime, hunger, disease, and scandals?[132]

Mishaps

• As a young man, Roy Bean—who was later known as Judge Roy Bean, the Law West of the Pecos—tried to go into the dairy business. He bought a herd of cows and a fleet of wagons, and he delivered milk daily. However, feed costs for the cows soared, so he gave the cows less feed, which caused them to give less milk. No problem. Mr. Bean started to water the milk to make it go further. Unfortunately, a customer on his route came to him one day and complained—he had found a minnow in his milk! Mr. Bean was properly shocked and said, "That's what I get for watering them cows down at the river."[133]

• In 1958, when Larry King first left Brooklyn and went to South Florida, he hit John F. Kennedy's car. Senator Kennedy was pretty steamed about it, saying, "How could you? Early Sunday morning, no traffic, not a cloud in the sky, I'm parked—how could you run into me?" Unfortunately, Mr. King did not have a good excuse—he had simply been gawking at the fancy Palm Beach boutiques. Mr. Kennedy did offer to forget about the accident—if Mr. King promised to vote for him in the Presidential election. Mr. King did, and Mr. Kennedy drove away—after telling Mr. King, "Stay waaay behind me."[134]

• When world-famous Barney's window-dresser Simon Doonan was growing up, his mother got dentures, as so many people did back then. Unfortunately, her dentures did not fit well, as so many people's dentures did not back then. One of Mr. Doonan's happiest memories is that of his mother sneezing and her dentures popping out of her mouth and skittering across the floor. This happened to lots of people other than Mr. Doonan's mother. He remembers, "Flying dentures were a common sight back then."[135]

• Robert Schumann wished to be a concert pianist, and he invented a device that he thought would help him develop independence in the fourth finger of his right hand. Unfortunately, the device crippled the finger, rendering it useless for playing the piano. As a consequence, he gave up his dream of being a great concert pianist and instead became a great Romantic composer.[136]

Money

• J. Edgar Hoover built his career on Americans' fear of Communism. On 2 January 1920, he was responsible for the arrest of 10,000 Americans suspected of being Communists, most of whom were found to be innocent and were released. These police-state tactics were widely condemned. In fact, few Americans have been

Communists. By 1971, the members of the Communist Party in America numbered only 2,800—but many of them were really FBI agents. In 1963, Hoover told the assistant secretary of the State Department, "If it were not for me, there would not even be a Communist Party, because I've financed the Communist Party in order to know what they're doing." FBI agent William Sullivan's duties included closely monitoring the Communist Party. He once suggested that Hoover release the membership numbers of the Communist Party in order to show Americans that the FBI was winning the war against subversion. Hoover refused to do so, asking, "How do you think I'm going to get my appropriations out of Congress if you keep downplaying the Communist Party?" After Hoover died, Mr. Sullivan said that the "Communist threat" was actually "a lie perpetrated on the American people."[137]

• During the Joseph McCarthy days of suppression of free speech, Studs Terkel was blacklisted, resulting in the cancellation of his early-TV show, *Stud's Place*, despite good ratings. He began to pick up money by making speeches—some of which were cancelled because of the social and political activism that had gotten him blacklisted. Edward Clamage of the Illinois American Legion often let the sponsors of Stud's speeches know that they were hiring someone who he thought was a "dangerous subversive." When the speech went on anyway, Mr. Terkel would write a letter to Mr. Clamage: "Clamage, it comes to my attention that you are at it once again. Thanks to you, my fee was raised from $100 to $200. I owe you an agent's fee." Studs adds, "It wasn't true, of course, but it made him furious. It was a way of getting back."[138]

• Gilbert Stuart was both a great artist and a spendthrift who could not pay his debts. Often, he would contract to paint a portrait, get paid in advance, then spend the money and not complete the portrait. In Dublin, Ireland, he was thrown into prison for nonpayment of debts. There, he continued to paint portraits—because he was in prison, he actually completed them and was able to earn enough money to get out of prison. Later, he painted some famous portraits of George Washington, but he always kept the original, painted copies, and sold the copies. He even gave President Washington a copy and kept the original for himself.[139]

• Rabbi Yose ben Kisma once met a man who discovered that the Rabbi came from a center of civilization filled with great scholars. After hearing that, the man offered Rabbi Yose much wealth—"a million gold dinars and precious stones and pearls"—to live in his city. However, Rabbi Yose immediately rejected the man's offer, saying, "Were you to give me all the silver and gold and precious stones and pearls in the world I would not live anywhere except in a place of Torah." How did the good Rabbi know that the man's city was not a place of Torah? Because money was the foremost topic in the man's conversation.[140]

• Early in the history of Microsoft, Ross Perot attempted to buy the company. He offered Bill Gates millions—somewhere between $6 million and $60 million. They couldn't come to an agreement, and Bill Gates kept his company—and became a billionaire. Later, Mr. Perot said, "I should have just said, 'Now, Bill, you set the price, and I'll take it.'"[141]

• Owen Cooper was loyal to his state of Mississippi. Once, he and country comedian Jerry Clower were driving from Tennessee back to Mississippi. Mr. Cooper was almost out of gas, but when Mr. Clower mentioned that fact to him, he replied, "I'm trying to make it back to Mississippi because my state will get several cents a gallon."[142]

• Sometimes, rich people give no money to charity. Rabbi Eizel Charif of Slonim once knew such a man, but said that the man did follow at least one of the rules of giving to charity. No one is required to give so much money that a poor man becomes rich, and the man had never been guilty of doing that.[143]

• Spalding Gray's monologue, *Swimming to Cambodia*, tells about American B-52s accidentally bombing a Cambodian village, causing loss of life and limbs. The USAmerican military responded by giving $100 to families that had suffered a death and $50 to people who had lost a leg or an arm.[144]

• During World War I, Enrico Caruso worked hard to raise money for the Allied effort. He once conducted an auction of some boxes of oranges and raised $47,000—Mr. Caruso himself bought one box of oranges for $4,000.[145]

• A woman once asked the ancient Greek poet Simonides which was better: to be wise or to be wealthy? He replied that it was better to be wealthy, for he often saw wise men sitting on the doorsteps of wealthy men.[146]

Mothers

• Juliette Gordon Low, founder of the Girl Scouts in 1912, was a very poor speller and chooser of words, as her letters—which included such spellings as *octabus*, *innocense*, and *vertuous*—showed. Once, her amused mother wrote her about an error in one of the letters she had received from her: "Please remember that a person's *bust* means *both their bosoms* and according to your descriptions of Alice's 'busts' the unfortunate child has four—two in front I suppose and two behind I conclude, which is certainly more than her share and no wonder her dress had to be let out."[147]

• Chaim Weizmann was a Zionist leader who became the first President of Israel. While Mr. Weizmann was fiercely advocating the establishment of Israel, a member of the British House of Lords asked him, "Why do you Jews insist on Palestine when there are so many undeveloped countries you could settle in more conveniently?" Mr. Weizmann replied, "That is like my asking you why you drove 20 miles to visit your mother last Sunday when there are so many old ladies living on your street."[148]

• Union organizer Cesar Chavez' mother, Juana, was a deeply moral woman. She used to send Cesar and Richard (his brother) out to find a homeless person and bring him home so she could give him a meal. One of the things that she taught her children was this Spanish saying: "It takes two to fight." One way to stop a fight is to prevent it in the first place by declining to fight.[149]

Chapter 4: From Music to Prejudice Music

• In 1939, African-American contralto Marian Anderson wanted to make her Washington, D.C., debut at Constitution Hall, but the Daughters of the American Revolution owned it and flatly refused to let her sing there. As a result, the DAR's most famous member, Eleanor Roosevelt, resigned, and Ms. Anderson gave an outdoor concert on Easter Sunday, April 9, in front of the Lincoln Memorial. She was introduced by Harold Ickes, the Secretary of the Interior, who said, "Genius draws no color line." Years later, she sang at Constitution Hall. Asked if she had forgiven the DAR, Ms. Anderson replied, "Ages and ages ago. You lose a lot of time hating people." Even later, her nephew, James DePreist, conducted an orchestra at Constitution Hall. For him, it was strictly routine. He parked his car there, rehearsed there, conducted there, and no one thought it was odd that he was an African American doing all these things.[150]

• Opera singer Ernestine Schumann-Heink learned just how famous she was when she visited what she called "a tumble-down hotel in a little one-horse town not even on the map." A resident asked her, "Say, ma'am, ain't you that big, fat, famous female singer whose face we're a seein' all the time in the newspaper?" Remarkably free of attitude, Ms. Schumann-Heink readily admitted that she was a big, fat, female singer, although she was surprised at being famous so far from a city.[151]

• Pyotr Ilich Tchaikovsky once agreed to write a piece of music a month for a publication, but he was afraid that he would forget to meet his obligation, so he told a servant to remind him each month when the piece was due. Unfortunately, his servant often told him, "Pyotr Ilich, tomorrow is the day," forcing Tchaikovsky to quickly write a piece of music. Still, the 12 pieces of music, collectively known as "The Seasons," are very listenable.[152]

• People have gotten upset over the violent lyrics in some rap music. Michael Moore, author of *Stupid White Men*, wonders why these people don't get upset over lyrics sung by Johnny Cash ("I shot a man in Reno / just to watch him die"), Bruce Springsteen ("I killed everything in my path / I can't say that I'm sorry for the things that we done"), or the Dixie Chicks ("Earl had to die").[153]

• Yousuf Karsh had the honor of photographing many, many great men and women and talking to them. When he took Albert Einstein's portrait, he asked the great scientist what the world would be like after another atomic bomb explosion. Mr. Einstein replied, "Alas, we will no longer be able to hear the music of Mozart."[154]

• The most famous song lyrics written by a lesbian are probably the lyrics for "America the Beautiful," written by Katherine Lee Bates (1859-1929), a Wellesley College professor who had a 25-year relationship with Katherine Coman, another professor at Wellesley. Ms. Bates wrote the lyrics originally as a poem titled "Pikes Peak." The music was written by Samuel A. Ward, a church organist and choirmaster.[155]

Names

• A man can keep his name alive in many ways. Perhaps the best way is to have children; however, another way is to have an institution of higher education named after you. In 1905, Moses Aaron Dropsie died. A Philadelphia lawyer, he left most of his estate to fund the founding of a college devoted especially to Hebrew studies. The governors of the new college discussed its name, and they wondered whether naming the college after Mr. Dropsie would put the new institution of higher learning at a disadvantage. However, when they reflected that Mr. Dropsie had no children, they decided to use the name Dropsie University.[156]

• The word "faggot," which is used to refer to gay people in a derogatory manner, may come from the word "fagot," which is a stick of wood burned in a fire. During the Middle Ages, people sometimes burned gays at the stake because they thought gays were dangerous. By the way, many famous people have been gay or bisexual, including composer Pyotr Tchaikovsky, painter Andy Warhol, playwright Tennessee Williams, tennis player Martina Navratilova, United Nations secretary-general Dag Hammarskjöld, and writers Hans Christian Andersen, James Baldwin, Willa Cather, and Gertrude Stein.[157]

• During the Gold Rush, drunken prospector James Finney, whom everyone called Old Virginny, staggered along a street in a town in Nevada one night and dropped a bottle of whiskey, smashing it. He then shouted, "I christen this ground Virginia." Quickly, the town became known as Virginia City. By the way, most miners in the Gold Rush made little or no money, as you can tell by looking at the names of old mining towns in the west: Bed Bug, Dry Diggings, Drytown, Mad Mule Gulch, Poverty Flat, and Rough and Ready.[158]

• The late investigative reporter I.F. Stone was Jewish. Because he was worried about fascism and anti-Semitism, and the possibility that they might come to the United States, he changed his name in 1937 from Isidor Feinstein to Gregory Stone and then to I.F. Stone. He later felt bad about having changed his name. By the way, Mr. Stone was contemptuous of spending money on gathering intelligence. He believed that even if the reports contained good information, American bureaucrats wouldn't read them. Why? "They don't like to read. They want everything on one piece of paper."[159]

• June 29, 1953, was "Maria Tallchief Day" in the famous ballerina's native state of Oklahoma. Among the honors she received that day was being given the title of "Commodore of the Oklahoma Navy." This title is strictly honorary—Oklahoma is land-locked and doesn't have a navy. Ms. Tallchief also attended a morning reception given for her by the Osage Tribal Council, where her grandmother Eliza gave her the name *Wa-Xthe-Thonba*, which means "Woman of Two Standards," in recognition of Ms. Tallchief's dual heritage of Osage Native American and white European.[160]

• Patrick Henry advocated the independence of America from the rule of Great Britain. On 23 March 1775, he made a famous speech that ended, "Is life so dear, or peace so sweet, as to be purchased at the price of chains and slavery? Forbid it, Almighty God! I know not what course others may take, but as for me, give me liberty or give me death!" The ending words so resonated with the American spirit that some soldiers had the words "LIBERTY OR DEATH" put on their uniforms. Such speeches also earned Mr. Henry the nickname "Son of Thunder."[161]

• The formal title "Dalai Lama," which was first used in the 1500s, means "Ocean of Wisdom." The current Dalai Lama, the 14th, has several names. When he became the Dalai Lama in a religious ceremony, he gave up the name he was given at birth: Lhamo Thondup. In lieu of his birth name, he assumed the name Jamphel Ngawang Lobsang Yeshe Tenzin Gyatso. Westerners usually call him either His Holiness the Dalai Lama or Tenzin Gyatso. Tibetans call him one of these names: Gyalwa Rinpoche, Yeshi Norbu, or Kundun.[162]

• Mahatma Gandhi's name at birth was Mohandas Gandhi. "Mohandas" means "Slave of Mohan"—"Mohan" is another name for the Hindu god Krishna. Gandhi was a member of the Vaisya caste, members of which are such things as merchants, clerks, and small landowners. "Gandhi" means "Grocer." "Mahatma," of course, means "Great Soul," but Gandhi was never comfortable with this name—which was given to him by people who recognized his spirituality.[163]

• African-American poet and playwright LeRoi Jones changed his name to the African name Imamu Ameer Baraka. *Imamu* means "spiritual leader." *Ameer* means "blessed." *Baraka* means "prince." Later, he adopted a shortened version of the name: Amiri Baraka. Also, Nikki Giovanni has a last name that seems unusual for an African-American poet, but she explains, "It just means that our slave masters were Italian instead of English or French."[164]

• Maria Tallchief's English name at birth was Elizabeth "Betty" Marie Tall Chief, but she changed it so it would sound more exotic and theatrical to balletomanes. An advantage in combining "Tall" and "Chief" is that the "-ief" ending resembled the ending "-ieff" found so often at the end of Russian names—however, the correct Russian form of her name would have been "Tallchieva."[165]

• George W. Bush is a social person, and he quickly gets to know people and names. He pledged Delta Kappa Epsilon at Yale, and at the pledge ceremony all of the pledges were asked to name as many people in the room as they could. Except for George, all of the pledges knew the names of four or five people. George knew the names of everybody in the room—all 54 of them.[166]

• When famous detective Allan Pinkerton built an estate at Onarga, Illinois, he named it "The Larches," and he imported 85,000 young larch trees from his native Scotland to plant there. By the way, Mr. Pinkerton enjoyed playing practical jokes. Often, he would take his guests out boating, then deliberately tip over the boat.[167]

Native Americans

• One of the beliefs of the Native Americans known as the Wampanoag is that each of us bears responsibility for protecting the environment. In fact, each generation is responsible for preserving the environment for the following seven generations. By the way, clambakes are a Wampanoag tradition. Sickissuogs are soft-shelled clams along the coast of New England that have a surprising behavior when they are removed from the sand in which they live. When 12-year-old Steven Peters, a member of the tribe, harvested some sickissuogs in preparation for a clambake, they sprayed seawater onto his face.[168]

• The largest Native American nation in 2020 was the Navajo Nation, which had 399,494 tribal members. The Navajo Reservation is also the largest in the United States. It is about the size of West Virginia and is composed of parts of the states of Arizona, New Mexico, and Utah. To cross by car from one side of the Navajo Reservation to the other takes about six hours. By the way, the traditional Navaho dwelling is an eight-sided building known as a hogan. The door of the hogan always faces east, so that in the morning the sun will shine through the doorway and wake everyone up.[169]

• When members of the Native American tribe of the Ojibway (also known as Chippewa) gather wild rice, their sacred food, they take only as much as they need. They know that the rest of the rice will be used. Birds will eat it, and it will provide the seed for next year's crop of wild rice. By the way, tobacco is regarded as sacred by many Native Americans. The Ojibway sometimes sprinkle tobacco on the rivers where wild rice grows. The tobacco is a gift to the Creator.[170]

• Chief Osceola and his tribe of Native Americans known as the Seminoles successfully resisted efforts by the United States government to move them to a reservation west of the Mississippi River. They journeyed deep into the Florida Everglades, where U.S. soldiers found it impossible to track them. For eight years, the U.S. government waged war to force the Seminoles out of the Everglades, but in 1842, it gave up. The Seminoles won, and they are still there.[171]

Peace

• In pre-Civil War Virginia, Seth Laughlin believed that slaves should be free. Because Quakers believed as he did, he became a Quaker. In Quaker meetings, he learned that Jesus valued peace. Jesus even said in his Sermon on the Mount, "Blessed are the peacemakers; for they shall be called the children of God." After the Civil War started, he was drafted—in 1863—into the Confederate Army. However, he stated that he was a pacifist due to his religious beliefs. An officer ordered him to stand for 36 hours—a soldier used a bayonet to keep him awake. They used other kinds of torture on Mr. Laughlin, including suspending him by his thumbs from a tree. Mr. Laughlin did not break. Eventually, he was court-martialed, found guilty, and sentenced to be executed. He asked for permission to pray before he was shot. After permission to pray was granted to him, he prayed for the people who were supposed to shoot him, "Father, forgive them, for they know not what they do." The soldiers refused to shoot him, and the officers of the military court changed his sentence to prison instead of death by firing squad. Due to the torture he had undergone, Mr. Laughlin fell ill and died in prison.[172]

• Actor Robert Clary survived a number of concentration camps, including Buchenwald, during the Holocaust. He is best known for playing the character of Corporal Louis LeBeau in the TV sitcom *Hogan's Heroes*, which is set in a prisoner-of-war camp during World War II. He lectures frequently about the Holocaust, and he creates art that depicts scenes of peace. Mr. Clary says, "My wish is that a hundred years from now when a teacher asks a student to face a map of the world, to close his eyes and point to a place on the map ... when that child opens his eyes, wherever he has pointed, that place in the world will be at peace ... no wars, no famine, no hatred."[173]

• Unfortunately, Ireland was a battleground between the Catholics and the Protestants for many centuries. The Irish flag has three strips. The orange stripe represents the minority Protestants, the green stripe represents the majority Catholics, and the white middle stripe represents hope—hope for union of the peoples of Ireland. Now Northern Ireland is a part of the United Kingdom, and the Republic of Ireland is a sovereign country. The 1998 Good Friday Agreement shared power between the two groups.[174]

People with Handicaps

• Nahara Rodriguez' legs were paralyzed in an automobile accident, but she learned to swim again. One of the operations she underwent was for the purpose of implanting electrodes in her legs. Because she was paralyzed, she had no feeling in her legs, so she did not need anesthesia and stayed awake for the operation, watching *Pinocchio* as the doctors did what doctors do during an operation. The electrodes helped her to stand up (a major accomplishment), but they had to be removed after her body began to reject them. In 1998, she won the Courage Award, which is given in honor of track-and-field athlete Wilma Rudolph. She also competed in the 1998 Miss Pennsylvania American Junior Teen Pageant, where she finished among the top 10 and also won "Miss Personality."[175]

• A man who had murdered his mother, her best friend, and six female hitchhikers spent part of his life sentence in prison recording books for the blind, including law textbooks for a blind man who became a lawyer. Why did he do that? He wanted to help people who were "less fortunate" than he was.[176]

Physicians

• William Harvey (1578-1652), who discovered how the blood circulates in the body, was able to see a live human heart. A boy had suffered an injury that opened his chest. The boy recovered, but the hole remained in his chest, and to protect himself he wore a metal plate over the hole. The boy became an adult, and Dr. Harvey met him and saw the hole in his chest. Dr. Harvey estimated that three fingers and a thumb could fit in the hole. A constantly moving part of the young man's body stuck out a little—it was the young man's heart. The young man allowed both Dr. Harvey and King Charles I of England to see his heart, and the king even touched the young man's heart. This did not cause the young man pain because the heart, like other internal organs, could not feel touch.[177]

• The United States' first doctor who was a woman was Elizabeth Blackwell. Although 29 medical schools rejected her application to be a student, she finally got in and graduated with a medical degree in 1849. Despite her degree, hospitals refused to hire her, so in 1857 she opened the New York Infirmary for Women and Children, hiring an all-woman staff.[178]

Politicians

• Satirist Michael Moore was gladdened in 1996 by the election defeat of Congressman Bob Dornan of Orange County, California. When Mr. Dornan filed suit claiming that the people voting for his opponent were illegal aliens, Mr. Moore attempted to file suit claiming that the people who voted for Mr. Dornan were insane. When asked for proof that these people were insane, Mr. Moore gave the fact that they had voted for Mr. Dornan. Mr. Moore once spoke with some mental health professionals about Bob Dornan, citing statements Mr. Dornan had made (such as comments about "homos" and a "disloyal, betraying little Jew") and actions Mr. Dornan had performed (Mr. Dornan once physically attacked fellow Congressman Tom Downey), but Mr. Moore did not reveal Mr. Dornan's name. The mental health professionals agreed that the man described was very likely mentally ill and possibly dangerous.[179]

• Amelia Earhart twice became the first woman to fly across the Atlantic Ocean—once as a passenger, and once as a solo pilot. Norwegian aviator Bernt Balchen, who became a consultant for her solo flight, asked Ms. Earhart if she thought that she could make the flight alone. She cheerfully replied, "You bet!" And she did make it. After 15 hours and 18 minutes in the air, she landed in a field near Londonderry, where she told a farmer that she had come from the United States. He didn't believe her, replying merely, "Have you now?"

One person who did believe her was Lady Nancy Astor, the first woman ever elected to Parliament. She sent Ms. Earhart a telegram: "Come stay with us, and I'll lend you a nightgown."[180]

• In the early 1970s, after Mickey Leland, an African-American, was elected to the Texas legislature, columnist Molly Ivins wondered whether this particular politician would make a difference. One of the first things she saw him do was stand in the middle of the natural amplifier known as the capitol rotunda and yell at some friends, "Godd*mnit, are you n*ggers comin' down to get lunch, or what?" He made a difference, working hard to pass legislation to benefit the people instead of big business.[181]

• Abraham Lincoln used to tell a story about a preacher giving a sermon that asserted that no perfect woman had ever existed on earth. However, a woman in the congregation arose and said that she knew of the existence of a perfect woman. The preacher asked who she was, and the woman answered, "My husband's first wife."[182]

• In 1992, then-President George H. W. Bush said in a public speech, "We need a nation closer to the Waltons than the Simpsons." Three days later, on *The Simpsons*, Bart said after he and his family watched the President attack them on television, "We're just like the Waltons. We're praying for an end to the depression, too."[183]

• While waiting for a flight at O'Hare Airport in Chicago, U.S. Representative James R. Jones (Oklahoma) freshened up in a restroom, where he noticed this message written above one of the hot-air machines used to dry hands: "Push here and get a message from your Congressman."[184]

Prayer

• Nathan Kalir (1824-1886) was sometimes so busy with political duties that he neglected to pray regularly, something that upset his wife very much. Once his political duties took him on a trip to a country where the winters were very cold. After he had unpacked and settled in, he wrote his wife that he could not find his long underwear, which he would need during the winter. His wife wrote back, "Pray to God, and your prayers will be answered." Mr. Kalir opened the prayer bag that held his prayer shawl and tefillin and discovered that his wife had also packed his long underwear there.[185]

• On 12 April 1945, Vice President Harry Truman learned that President Franklin Roosevelt had died. He understood the enormity of the job he was facing, and the next morning, on his first full day as President, he looked at three reporters and told them, "Boys, the moon and the stars fell on me. If you ever prayed before, pray for me."[186]

• Want to say a prayer in the Winnebago (Native American) language? Just say *Myoona* (Great Spirit) *Peenagee-gee* (Thank you). When you're hungry, this prayer has the advantage of being only two words long.

Prejudice

• In high school, Martin Luther King, Jr. demonstrated remarkable public-speaking skills. Once, he and one of his teachers traveled on a segregated bus to another town so Martin could give a speech. They sat in the back—as required by law. The law also required blacks to stand up and offer their seats to whites when the bus got full. However, when the bus got full, Martin declined to stand up. The bus driver threatened to have him arrested, but Martin held his ground until his teacher asked him to stand up and give up his seat to a white person. Martin and his teacher stood up during the 90-mile trip. Later, as part of his nonviolent resistance to unjust laws, Martin Luther King, Jr. was arrested many times and taken to jail. When his children were small, they would ask their mother, "Why is Daddy in jail?" Coretta Scott King would answer, "Daddy is helping people."[187]

• Marian Wright Edelman, an African American, witnessed prejudice at first hand while growing up in Bennettsville, South Carolina. On a highway in front of her home, a truck driven by a white man collided with a car filled with a black migrant worker's family. An ambulance arrived, but the white driver of the ambulance examined the white man, said that he was fine, then drove off, leaving behind the badly injured black victims. Ms. Edelman says, "I remember watching children like me bleeding. I remember the ambulance driving off. You never, ever forget." In 1973, Ms. Edelman founded the Children's Defense Fund, which lobbies politicians to pass legislation to help children.[188]

• Making *Jungle Fever*, about the romance between a black man and an Italian-American woman, was difficult. Filmmaker Spike Lee directed some scenes of the movie in the largely Italian neighborhood of Bensonhurst in Brooklyn. The inspiration for the movie was the murder of Yusef Hawkins by a white mob in Bensonhurst in 1989. While making the movie, Mr. Lee received three bomb threats, and he, actor Wesley Snipes, and his cameraman had rocks thrown at them. One of the rocks actually hit the cameraman, Ernest Dickerson. For a while, the people making the movie had to be guarded by police officers.[189]

• On 19 April 1995, a bomb exploded in front of the Alfred P. Murrah Federal Building in Oklahoma City, Oklahoma, causing the deaths of 168 people, including nineteen children. Some people immediately assumed that Arab terrorists had caused the bombing, and some people of Arab descent found themselves the target of prejudice. They were harassed by citizens not of Arab descent, and they were arrested and taken in for questioning by the police. Some people of Arab descent even feared for their lives. Later, a white American named Timothy McVeigh was convicted of the crime.[190]

• As a result of the Supreme Court's decision in *Brown v. Topeka (Kansas) Board of Education*, schools were forced to desegregate. In Boston, protests by white parents broke out, and the parents' racial hatred infected their children. Richie Wallace, a black junior high school student, reported that everyday when the black students got off the bus, white students called them racial slurs and threatened them. Older white students sometimes made younger white students run down the school hallways wearing white sheets and yelling, "The Klansmen are coming!"[191]

• When civil-rights activist Fannie Lou Hamer was growing up, her family was very poor and worked as sharecroppers. At one point, it seemed as if her family would be able to pull themselves out of poverty. Her father got enough money together to rent some land, tools, and animals. Unfortunately, a white man deliberately poisoned their mules and cows. Ms. Hamer says, "He couldn't stand to see [African-Americans] doing all right. We went right back to the bottom again, and that's where we stayed—sharecropping."[192]

• Major-league pitcher Bob Gibson was born in Omaha, Nebraska, and he did not care for his first stay in the Deep South when he was a minor-league player in Columbus, Georgia. A fan called him "Alligator Bait," and later Mr. Gibson discovered what that meant. According to Mr. Gibson, "Negro kids used to be tied to the end of a rope and dragged through the swamps to attract alligators. The Negro kid would be pulled out of the water and onto the shore, and the alligator would come out of the water after him. Then they would catch the alligator." (Let's hope this is a rural legend.)[193]

• African-American singer Marian Anderson married Orpheus "King" Fisher, who was also African-American, but who was so light skinned that he could pass for white. Once, he went shopping for a house for himself and his wife. He found the perfect house, and signs looked extremely good for his purchasing it, but when the real estate agent saw Ms. Anderson, the price jumped up suddenly. Even though the Fishers were willing to pay thousands of dollars more for the house, the real estate agent finally told them that they couldn't buy it at any price because they weren't white.[194]

• The parents of Penn Jillette of Penn and Teller fame were good people. They went to a church in Massachusetts, and the minister was

Pastor Shirley, who lived with a female friend, a fact that started lots of rumors that she was a lesbian—rumors that got her kicked out as minister of that church. Penn's parents believed in privacy, and they did not care to speculate about Pastor Shirley's sexuality, but other members of the church seemed to spend quite a lot of time doing just that. Penn's parents donated generously to the church, making and keeping an annual pledge. When Pastor Shirley was kicked out of the church, Penn's parents stopped attending church, but they still sent in their pledges until the end of the pledge period. Penn's sister and brother-in-law did the same thing. After the pledge period was over, Penn's sister took the money that she and her husband had budgeted for the church and did other good deeds with it, such as buying jaws of life for ambulances and bulletproof vests for the local police.[195]

• Some people enjoy hating gays. A minister named Fred Phelps is a person like that—he goes to the funerals of gay men and displays signs saying things like this: "God Hates Faggots." When he came to Boulder, Colorado, many gays protested his message. They carried their own signs, such as "Beware of Unsafe Sects." One gay man even carried the sign, "I am Fred Phelps' Love Slave." Still, Phelps' group carried its own signs, including one saying "Hate is a Bible Value." Such hatred is harmful. Bobby Griffith came from a religious family that told him that gay men would go to hell because they were sinful. On 27 August 1983, Mr. Griffith, a gay man, committed suicide two months after his 20th birthday by jumping from a freeway overpass directly in front of a fast-moving truck.[196]

• When she was 17 years old, Alice Walker got on board a bus in the South to travel to Spelman College in Atlanta, Georgia, where she would take classes. A white woman complained because Ms. Walker was sitting near the front of the bus, and the bus driver forced her to move, but Ms. Walker vowed to fight such prejudice. In Atlanta, she became active in the Civil Rights Movement, and throughout her life she has been a force for freedom.[197]

• George Takei, who played Mr. Hikaru Sulu on the original *Star Trek* TV series, grew up in American internment camps for Japanese-Americans during World War II. He had a teacher who referred to him as "that little Jap boy," and each morning, he was able to look out the school window and see barbed-wire fences and guard towers as he ended the Pledge of Allegiance by reciting "with justice and liberty for all."[198]

• When Martin Luther King, Jr., was young, he and his father went to a shoe store to make a purchase, but the white clerk said that for them to be served they would have to go to the back of the store. Martin's father declined to do that, and they left without purchasing anything. Martin remembers his father saying about Jim Crow that day, "I don't care how long I have to live with this system, I am never going to accept it. I'll oppose it to the day I die."[199]

• When Coretta Scott was growing up in Marion, Alabama, in the 1930s, black children were discriminated against. White children could order whatever flavor of ice cream they wanted at the drugstore, but black children had to eat whatever flavor of ice cream the drugstore wanted to get rid of.[200]

• Albert Asriyan was an Armenian songwriter whose songs were heard often on television in the Soviet Union. However, because of prejudice against the Armenians, Mr. Asriyan's name sometimes did not appear on the credits of the television programs featuring his music.[201]

• In 1959, actor John Hurt was an art student living in London. At the time, prejudice was openly displayed, and people who rented rooms often advertised with signs that read, "Coloureds and Irish need not apply."[202]

Presidents

• Ohio Senator Benjamin Wade once criticized President Abraham Lincoln when the president tried to tell him an anecdote. Senator Wade told the President, "It is nothing but anecdotes. I have heard enough of them. You are letting the country go to hell on anecdotes. We are not more than a mile from there now." President Lincoln replied, "Mr. Wade, that is just about the distance to the Capitol, isn't it?"[203]

    • President Lyndon B. Johnson was thought to have an huge ego. German Chancellor Ludwig Erhard once said to him, "I understand, Mr. President, that you were born in a log cabin." President Johnson replied, "No, you have me confused with Lincoln. I was born in a manger."[204]

Chapter 5: From Problem-Solving to Work

Problem-Solving

• What happened in South Africa after apartheid ended? It could have been a bloodbath. Some whites had murdered people in the Sharpeville Massacre. Some whites had tortured and murdered political prisoners. Some blacks had necklaced—hung a tire around someone's neck and then set the tire on fire—blacks who were suspected of collaborating with white people. A bloodbath could have been the revenge for these acts. Instead, Archbishop Desmond Tutu became the leader of the Truth and Reconciliation Commission, which held hearings throughout South Africa. Movie critic Roger Ebert describes the rules of the Commission in this way: "Describe fully what you did, who your victims were, and where their bodies might be found, and then make an apology that the Commission members believed. Then walk away. Your crimes and your sins are now between you and heaven." The Commission worked. White South Africans and black South Africans were dead tired of violence, and they were eager to end the violence.[205]

• The 14th Dalai Lama recognized the isolation of Tibet and was determined to learn about modern things. The 13th Dalai Lama had owned all the automobiles that existed in Tibet—four—and so the 14th Dalai Lama determined to get them running and to learn to drive them. With the help of a car-knowledgeable Tibetan named Tashi Tsering, three of the cars were put in working order, and one day when Mr. Tsering was absent, the 14th Dalai Lama started one of the cars and drove around a garden. Unfortunately, he hit a tree and smashed a headlight. Not wanting Mr. Tsering to know that he had driven one of the cars, the 14th Dalai Lama found replacement glass for the headlight. Since the headlight had been tinted, and the replacement glass was not tinted, he coated it with sugar syrup until the color matched the tint of the original headlight.[206]

• Figure skater Sonja Henie was photographed shaking hands with Adolf Hitler at the 1936 Olympic Games. This came in handy when the Nazis were bearing down on her house in Norway. Knowing that the Nazis were coming, Ms. Henie ordered that the photograph be displayed prominently in her house. When the Nazis saw the photograph, they refrained from looting her house. (Although the photograph came in handy at that time, many Norwegians resented it, especially after Ms. Henie declined to contribute money to the Norwegian Resistance, saying that she was no longer a Norwegian but a USAmerican. Many Norwegians never forgave her for her lack of support during the war.)[207]

• Minneapolis-St. Paul, Minnesota, has a large number of Native Americans among its residents. Native Americans there were arrested much more often than members of other races, and the Native Americans felt that they were being singled out because of their race. In the late 1960s, Dennis Banks and other leaders of the American Indian Movement, an activist organization advocating civil rights for Native Americans, started street patrols to keep tabs on the police. They filmed arrests of Native Americans, and they advised Native Americans of their legal rights. Quickly, fewer Native Americans were arrested.[208]

• In 1974, Arthur Frye attended church, but instead of listening to the preacher, he let his mind wander. One problem he thought about was how to quickly open his hymnbook to the right hymn. He used pieces of paper as bookmarks for the hymns to be sung during service, but sometimes one or more pieces of paper would fall out of the hymnbook. He remembers, "It was during the sermon that I first thought, 'What I really need is a little bookmark that will stick to the paper but will not tear the paper when I remove it.'" This idea, of course, was solved when he became co-creator of Post-it Notes.[209]

• Julie-Anna Asriyan, an Armenian, used to live in Azerbaijan at a time when great hostility existed between the Armenians and the Azeris. She and her family used to go to bed at night with all their clothes on. That way, if there was an emergency—such as a firebombing or a gang of thugs breaking and entering into their home—they could leave quickly and still have clothes to wear. Fortunately, young Julie-Anna and her family moved to New York City, where they felt safe.[210]

• While carrying their boats and supplies around the Great Falls of the Missouri River, members of the Lewis and Clark expedition were greatly bothered by jagged rocks along the falls. They had to repair their moccasins at night, and every two days they were forced to make new moccasins. By the way, members of the Lewis and Clark expedition carried much food, including 193 pounds of dried soup, with them during their 1804-1806 journey of discovery in the American West.[211]

• After Ludwig van Beethoven's mother died, his father turned to alcohol, preferring to use his salary to get drunk rather than to buy food to feed his family. Therefore, Beethoven went to his father's employer and arranged that half of his father's salary each payday be paid to him instead of to his father so he could make sure the family had food to eat.[212]

• American artist Winslow Homer painted many seascapes, but the wind that blew on the Maine coast as he painted was very cold. To solve the problem of painting in a very cold wind, Mr. Homer created a portable painter's studio on wheels. He moved it to the scene he wanted to paint, and painted inside the studio, where there was a stove for heat.[213]

• Gays and lesbians are aware that they are often the targets of violence and hate. Therefore, they sometimes form safety patrols. For example, participating in the 1995 Gay Pride Day Parade in Chicago was a group called the Pink Angels Safety Patrol.[214]

• Japanese ninjas were very clever at assassinating people. One ninja learned that an enemy habitually went into his garden in the morning to smell the flowers, so at night the ninja went to the garden and sprinkled poison powder in the flower blossoms.[215]

• During World War II, a Jewish refugee was on a ship fleeing Germany and heading for freedom. On top of his dresser, the refugee kept a photograph of Adolf Hitler. When he was asked why, he replied, "It's to prevent homesickness."[216]

• King Hassan II of Morocco enjoyed golf, so he had his own golf course with 43 bunkers built. Unfortunately, the king kept hitting the ball into the bunkers. No problem. The king ordered the bunkers filled in and covered with grass.[217]

• In the old days, people who had need of a wooden leg sometimes made their own. Having a wooden leg was helpful in solving the problem of socks that tend to fall down. One gentleman simply tacked his sock to his wooden leg.[218]

• Muhammad, the prophet of Islam, was a great general. Leading an army of 10,000 soldiers, he ordered each man to build a campfire. The 10,000 campfires made his army appear bigger than it really was.[219]

Public Speaking

• On 29 May 1765, Patrick Henry made a famous speech against King George III of England. Mr. Henry was a major force in favor of American independence from Great Britain, and he orated, "Caesar had his Brutus! Charles the First his Cromwell! And George the Third …." At this point, people yelled at Mr. Henry to be quiet. Brutus had assassinated Caesar, and Cromwell had helped bring about the death of Charles I. If Mr. Henry were to advocate the assassination of George III, he could be killed as a traitor to the crown. However, Mr. Henry ended his sentence by saying, "And George the Third may profit by their example." In the sentence, he had not directly advocated the assassination of George the Third, yet an implicit threat was definitely present.[220]

• Some politicians are capable of wit. In 1976, Bob Dole was nominated to run for Vice President with Jerry Ford. Very quickly, he found himself making an acceptance speech on national TV. He thought his speech was pretty good, especially considering the limited amount of time he had to write it, but when he asked his mother how he had done, she replied, "You usually do better." Hubert Humphrey was known for making very long speeches. Once he was asked to speak for only 12 minutes, and he said, "The last time I spoke for only 12 minutes was when I said hello to my mother." While running for the Senate in 1964, Robert Kennedy said, "People say I am ruthless. I am not ruthless. And if I find the man who is calling me ruthless, I shall destroy him."[221]

• In 1910, Franklin Delano Roosevelt campaigned for New York state senator. He gave several speeches a day, and he traveled from place to place in a rented bright red Maxwell touring car. Frequently he traveled at what many people regarded as a dangerous speed—22 miles per hour.[222]

• A Member of Parliament named Mr. Paling interrupted one of Winston Churchill's speeches by yelling, "Dirty dog." Mr. Churchill simply smiled and told him, "This Honourable Member knows what dirty dogs do to palings." (A "paling" is a fence.)[223]

Pulitzer Prize

• *To Kill a Mockingbird* almost did not get written. Author Harper Lee was working on the manuscript when she got so frustrated that she opened a window and threw the manuscript out into the snowy slush. Then, crying, she telephoned her editor, Theresa van "Tay" Hohoff, who made her retrieve the manuscript. She finished the novel, which won the Pulitzer Prize and became one of the most popular novels of the 20th century although it is controversial because it depicts a racist society.[224]

• When Alice Walker, an African American, was four years old, her sharecropper parents were ready to put her in school, but their white landlord felt that young Alice should be working in the fields since no African-American child needed to go to school. Alice's mother had a forceful talk with the white landlord, and Alice attended school. Many years later, Ms. Walker won the Pulitzer Prize for her novel *The Color Purple*.[225]

Royalty

• Annie, the daughter of famous Canadian painter Jean-Paul Lemieux, was occasionally introduced as "the daughter of our beloved artist, Lemieux." She used to protest, "While I'm proud to be the daughter, how nice it would be if I were introduced on my own." Elizabeth, the Queen of England, and her consort, Prince Philip, were present—Prince Philip said, "And now you can understand how I often feel."[226]

• When Queen Elizabeth I realized that age was ruining her beauty, she tried to hide that fact by wearing thick makeup and red wigs. When that failed, she banned mirrors from her palace. By the way, when Sir Walter Raleigh founded the first English colony in the New World, he named it Virginia to honor Queen Elizabeth I, aka the Virgin Queen.[227]

• Camillien Houde was the long-time mayor of Montreal. Once, he and King George of England appeared together on a balcony at City Hall, and the throngs down below thundered their applause. Mayor Camillien turned to King George and said, "Sir, part of this enthusiasm is for you, also."[228]

Saint Patrick's Day

• Some places celebrate St. Patrick's Day in spectacular ways. People in Chicago change the color of the Chicago River to green on

St. Patrick's Day. Also, people in San Antonio, Texas, do the same thing to the color of the San Antonio River.[229]

Slavery

• One of the very earliest sculptures of Abraham Lincoln is at the top of a totem pole. In the 19th century, the Native American Tlingit tribe in southeastern Alaska was divided into two hostile factions: the Ravens and the Eagles. The United States bought Alaska from the Soviet Union in 1867 and established a fort on Tongass Island in 1868. The Eagles warred on the Ravens who lived on Tongass Island and were at the point of making them slaves when the Ravens went to the fort to ask for help. The commander of the fort met with leaders of both the Ravens and the Eagles and explained that the American flag now flew over Alaska. He also explained that Lincoln had earlier signed the Emancipation Proclamation and that slavery was now illegal. To honor Lincoln for saving his people from slavery, Chief Ebbetts of the Ravens decided to erect a totem pole to him, so he hired an artist named Thleda from a neighboring tribe, the Tsimshian, to carve the totem pole. Working from a photograph, Thleda placed the sculpture of a top-hatted Lincoln at the very top of the totem pole.[230]

• When Sam Clemens was young, he complained to his mother about the singing of a young slave boy. His mother's eyes filled with tears, and she explained to Sam that she was glad to hear the slave boy sing, because then she knew that he wasn't remembering being separated from his mother, who had been sold away from their town. Sam grew up to become better known as Mark Twain, author of the anti-slavery novel titled *Adventures of Huckleberry Finn*.[231]

• After the Civil War, a new species of poetry became popular. Poems in the "plantation tradition" presented blacks as happy when they had been slaves and sorry that they had been freed.[232]

Sports

• On 20 September 1973, Billie Jean King and Bobby Riggs met in a tennis match played in the Astrodome in Houston, Texas. The match came about because of the braggadocio of Mr. Briggs, who enjoyed making outrageous bets and playing matches in which he was handicapped by carrying a heavy suitcase in one hand or by holding a leash chained to a dog as he played. In this case, the 55-year-old Riggs challenged a woman tennis pro who was 25 years younger than he. The match was filled with hoopla. Mr. Riggs entered the stadium in a cart pulled by six beautiful women, while Ms. King entered while riding on a chair carried by handsome men. Before the match, the two competitors exchanged gifts. Mr. Riggs gave the "girl" a lollipop, while Mr. King gave the male chauvinist a piglet. Of course, Ms. King defeated Mr. Riggs in a match televised in 36 countries—she also won $100,000 in prize money.[233]

• As a child, Trent Dimas competed both in soccer and in gymnastics. But eventually he had to decide between the two sports—the state gymnastics meet and the state soccer championships were scheduled during the same weekend. His parents let him decide, and he chose gymnastics. This was a good decision, since he won a gold medal on the high bar at the 1992 Olympics in Barcelona. Mr. Dimas became the first Hispanic-American gymnast to win an Olympic gold medal, he was the only American men's gymnast to win a medal at the Barcelona Olympics. Today he does good deeds as a spokesperson for the National Hispanic Scholarship Fund and as a sponsor of several college scholarships for Latino scholars.[234]

Travel

• World traveler Diana Silbergeld has taught English in Thailand. On her first day of teaching, in a village far from anywhere, she managed to teach her students the English words for such objects as desks and other things that can be found in a classroom. In addition, she taught the students a few simple sentences in English. At the end of the lesson, the students presented her with some flowers and said one of the sentences she had taught them: "We are sad."[235]

• In 1947, Australian Harry Scott put an "Out to Lunch" sign on his Sydney door, then he and his wife, Oceana, set off on a here-and-there-about-the-world voyage in a boat that he had built. The trip lasted nine years, but they made it home safely.[236]

War

• During World War II, a sailor found a dog, drunk, lying in a gutter. The sailor smuggled the dog on board the Coast Guard cutter *Campbell*, and the dog, now named Sinbad, charmed everyone so much that the ship's captain allowed him to stay on board. Sinbad was given his own bunk, his data was entered into personnel files, and his name was called during roll call—he yipped when he heard his name. Sinbad did like alcohol, and after being discovered drunk, he was given a trial, and his rank was lowered from Chief Dog to First Class Dog. During battles against German U-boats, he stayed on deck. He retired in 1948, and at a reunion in 1986, his human crewmates remembered that as long as Sinbad served on the ship, none of the sailors on the *Campbell* was killed in battle. A reader wrote the author of this book to say that Sinbad was, and still is, legendary within the service. While there are no dogs aboard cutters now, many Coast Guard stations have them as official crew members. Another dog, who was named Onyx, recently deceased, was itself legendary in Michigan's Straits of Mackinac area.[237]

• War can be horrible. After the first Battle of Bull Run, doctors saved as many wounded soldiers as they could, performing amputations as needed. Working with the doctors were Sisters of Charity nuns, who served as nurses. The nurses worked hard, and late at night they went to bed, although Sister Blanche remarked that sleeping would be difficult because of "the odor of death about this place." In the morning, the odor was worse, and it was coming from the room next to where the nuns had slept. Sister Blanche courageously entered the room and found three amputated legs lying on the floor. They were buried, but in a coffin with a dead soldier. One of the Sisters of Charity wrote in her journal, "Yesterday a man was buried with three legs."[238]

• The mother of Ramones bass player Dee Dee Ramone had a rough life as a young German citizen in Germany during World War II. When Dee Dee was a child, his military family was stationed in Berlin, and he remembers how happy he was to discover an indoor swimming pool. He wanted his mother to go swimming with him, but she had endured three years of bombing attacks on the city. The war ended when she was 14, and she had buried many, many corpses by then. He told her about the pool, "Mom, it's great. Why don't you come swimming there with me?" She replied, "Because I remember that pool after the war. It was filled with blood from the bodies of dead horses and dead people."[239]

• The Second Punic War started after the Romans became worried when the Carthaginian general Hannibal captured the city of Saguntum in Spain. According to the Roman historian Livy, several Roman leaders, including Fabius, traveled to Carthage to demand that the Carthaginians either give them Hannibal or face war. The Carthaginians refused to hand over Hannibal, so Fabius said, "We bring you peace and war. Take what you will." The Carthaginians answered, "Whichever you please—we do not care." Fabius then said, "We give you war," and the Carthaginians, unmoved, replied, "We accept it."[240]

• Country comedian Jerry Clower has a brother named Sonny who is a retired Navy war hero. Once, Sonny complained about hearing "Rambo! Rambo!" all the time from his grandson. He asked who Rambo was, and in answer to the question, he and his grandson went to a movie starring Sylvester Stallone as Rambo. Jerry asked his brother what he thought about Rambo, and Sonny replied, "I was in a pretty tough outfit when I fought a war. If Rambo had been in my unit in the Navy, he'd have been a cook."[241]

• Even though their days of glory were over, the Spartans resisted King Philip II of Macedon, the father of Alexander the Great, who conquered Persia. Philip II once sent a message to the Spartans, asking whether he should come to them as a friend or as an enemy. The Spartans sent back the reply, "Neither!" Because Philip II wanted peace and not war with the Spartans, he wisely left the Spartans alone, although he did make sure that he controlled the areas surrounding Sparta.[242]

• Colin Powell, a four-star general, is of course a highly successful African-American. At a White House dinner, an African-American waiter said to him, "I just want to thank you and say it's been good to see you here. I was in World War II, and I fought all the way from North Africa to Italy." General Powell replied, "I should thank you."[243]

• During World War II, Holland thought that one way to delay the Nazis if they invaded would be to blow up the dikes and flood the land. Winston Churchill heard about the plan and cabled, "Hold Your Water Till The Jerries Come.—W.C."[244]

Weddings

• In Renaissance Italy, when women got married, parents used to give a dowry—money and goods—to their daughters' husbands. This could be expensive, and a family with lots of daughters could have trouble providing dowries. However, in Florence, a family with limited financial means could plan ahead and become a member of a dowry bank. Each time a daughter was born, the father could buy stock in a dowry bank, then wait 15 years and have enough money to pay the dowry.[245]

• Little Richard occasionally interrupted his singing career to serve God as a preacher. He officiated at the weddings of Bruce Willis and

Demi Moore, of Cindy Lauper, and of Little Stephen (guitarist for Bruce Springsteen).[246]

Work

• Sidney Weinberg, who was born in 1891, started at Goldman Sachs as an assistant to the janitor, then worked his way up to senior partner. He sat on the boards of directors of many companies, and he attended many, many meetings. At one meeting, many, many statistics were read out loud, and when the reciter of statistics paused briefly, Mr. Weinberg jumped up and yelled, "BINGO!" Mr. Weinberg could be irreverent when he felt he had adequate cause to be irreverent. During World War II, the Admiral Jean-François Darlan, who was an important Vichy official (the Vichy government of southern France collaborated with the Nazis) visited the White House. The American government had to treat the Admiral with respect due to the protocol of diplomacy. Mr. Weinberg, who was not a member of the government, although he was a visitor to the White House that day, did not. When he was ready to leave the White House, Mr. Weinberg gave the Admiral, who was wearing a flashy uniform, a quarter and told him, "Here, boy, get me a cab."[247]

• On June 5, 1878, Dorotea Arango, who became known in history as Pancho Villa, was born in Rio Grande in Durango, Mexico. His parents worked on the Hacienda del Rio Grande. When he was 16 years old, he was working as a peon or day laborer. Because he was ambitious, when he saw a chance to improve his life and make more money by working at the Hacienda del Norte, he took it. However, he did not first get permission from the owner of the Hacienda del Rio Grande. Because he did not have permission to take a different job, what he did was illegal and he was severely punished for his independence. He was captured and forced to run barefoot behind a horse all the way back to the Hacienda del Rio Grande, where he was severely flogged. Because of this, he became a bandit and later a leader of a revolutionary army.[248]

• Mining gold in the Klondike was arduous work; in fact, just getting to the Klondike was arduous work. Prospectors had to haul a ton of supplies over the Chilkoot Pass, or risk running out of food, but they were unable to carry more than 80 pounds over the pass at a time. One miner carried a ton of supplies over the pass, then made his way to Lake Lindemann. He built a boat there, then lost all his supplies when the boat crashed while running down the rapids. The miner then started over. He bought another ton of supplies, carried the supplies over the Chilkoot Pass, made his way to Lake Lindemann, and built another boat. Unfortunately, he again lost all his supplies when this boat crashed while running down the rapids. This time, the miner shot himself and died.[249]

• Famous detective Allan Pinkerton served as a spy and did intelligence work during the Civil War. Unfortunately, he consistently overestimated the size of Confederate forces, leading General George McClellan to be overly cautious. Mr. Pinkerton's sources included very frightened men who overestimated Confederate forces, and he took their inaccurate reports at face value. Still, he did some good in his life. His hatred of slavery led him to become involved with the Underground Railroad, and he was an early advocate of using women operatives in the detective business. Unfortunately, although he had been a workingman who had supported unions when he was a young man, his agency was used to protect strikebreakers and to bust unions when he was old.[250]

• Lots of black people were arrested, especially from 1955-1965, for engaging in activism to get their civil rights. Sometimes, they were told that their jail record would follow them around for the rest of their lives. Towanner Hinkle was 16 years old in 1965 when she participated in the demonstrations of Selma, Alabama, and yes, she was arrested many, many times during the Civil Rights Movement. Often, at job interviews people asked her if she has ever been to jail. She replied, "Yes, I've been to jail lots of times." The interviewers would look at her funny until she explained, "I went to jail for marching with the movement." Then the interviewers would relax and say, "Oh, don't even worry about that."[251]

• As a young adult, Henny Youngman picked up extra cash by working as a summons server, and he took great pride in serving warrants on hard-to-find characters. Once, he spent weeks trying to serve a summons on one man, only to succeed after noticing that the man had an office with a telephone near a window. On a hot day, when the windows were up (this was before air conditioning), Mr. Youngman called the man from a nearby pay phone and told him, "I've got some money for you. Can you hold on a minute?" The character held, Mr. Youngman walked across the street, reached in the open window, and put the summons in the man's vest pocket.[252]

• When photographer Margaret Bourke-White received permission to cover the 1942 Allied invasion of Tunisia during World War II, she thought that she would fly there. However, General Jimmy Doolittle, who commanded the Eighth Air Force, told her that she would be safer if she sailed there in a convoy. Ironically, a German torpedo struck her ship, but fortunately, she escaped in a lifeboat—and came away from the wreckage with some astonishing photographs.[253]

Appendix A: Bibliography

Aitkens, Maggi. *Kerry, a Teenage Mother*. Minneapolis, MN: Lerner Publications Company, 1994.

Alonso, Karen. Loving v. Virginia: *Interracial Marriage*. Berkeley Heights, NJ: Enslow Publications, Inc., 2000.

Anderson, Catherine Corley. *Jackie Kennedy Onassis: Woman of Courage*. Minneapolis, MN: Lerner Publications Company, 1995.

Aurand, Jr., A. Monroe. *Wit and Humor of the Pennsylvania Germans*. Harrisburg, PA: The Author, 1946.

Bailey, Paul, editor. *The Stately Homo: A Celebration of the Life of Quentin Crisp*. London: Bantam Press, 2000.

Banfield, Susan. *Ethnic Conflicts in School*. Springfield, NJ: Enslow Publications, Inc., 1995.

Bankston, John. *Sigmund Freud: Exploring the Mysteries of the Mind*. Berkeley Heights, NJ: Enslow Publishers, Inc., 2006.

Barnstone, Willis, translator. *Greek Lyric Poetry*. New York: Schocken Books, 1967.

Barreca, Regina, editor. *New Perspectives on Women and Comedy*. Philadelphia, PA: Gordon and Breach, 1992.

Bernotas, Bob. *Spike Lee: Filmmaker*. Hillside, NJ: Enslow Publications, Inc., 1993.

Block, Gay, and Malka Drucker. *Rescuers: Portraits of Moral Courage in the Holocaust*. New York: Holmes and Meier Publishers, Inc., 1992.

Bono, Chastity. *Family Outing*. With Billie Fitzpatrick. Boston, MA: Little, Brown and Company, 1998.

Boo, Michael. *The Story of Figure Skating*. New York: William Morrow and Company, 1998.

Breckenridge, W.K. *Anecdotes of Great Musicians*. New York: Pageant Press, Inc., 1955.

Broadwater, Andrea. *Marian Anderson: Singer and Humanitarian*. Berkeley Heights, NJ: Enslow Publications, Inc., 2000.

Calzo, Nick Del, creator and photographer. *The Triumphant Spirit*. Denver, CO: Triumphant Spirit Publishing, 1997.

Chadwick, Roxane. *Anne Morrow Lindbergh: Pilot and Poet*. Minneapolis, MN: Lerner Publications Company, 1987.

Chaliapine, Feodor Ivanovitch. *Pages From My Life: An Autobiography*. Trans. H.M. Buck. New York and London: Harper and Brothers, Publishers, 1927.

Cheatham, Kae. *Dennis Banks: Native American Activist*. Springfield, NJ: Enslow Publications, Inc., 1997.

Chernow, Ron. *The Death of the Banker*. New York: Vintage Books, 1997.

Claus, S. *Holiday Cheer for the 19th Hole*. With help from Russ Edwards and Jack Kreismer. Saddle River, NJ: Red-Letter Press, 2003.

Clower, Jerry. *Stories From Home*. Jackson, MI: University Press of Mississippi, 1992.

Cole, Michael D. *The* Titanic*: Disaster at Sea*. Berkeley Heights, NJ. Enslow Publications, Inc., 2001.

Cranston, Toller. *Zero Tollerance*. With Martha Lowder Kimball. Toronto, Canada: McClelland and Stewart, Inc., 1997.

Crutcher, Chris. *King of the Mild Frontier*. New York: Greenwillow Books, 2003.

Davis, Mary L. *Women Who Changed History: Five Famous Queens of Europe*. Minneapolis, MN: Lerner Publications Company, 1974.

Deane, Bill. *Bob Gibson*. New York: Chelsea House Publishers, 1994.

Dole, Bob. *Great Political Wit*. New York: Doubleday, 1998.

Dole, Bob. *Great Presidential Wit*. New York: Scribner, 2001.

Doonan, Simon. *Nasty*. New York: Simon & Schuster, 2005.

Dosick, Rabbi Wayne. *The Business Bible: Ten Commandments for Creating an Ethical Workplace*. New York: William Morrow and Company, Inc., 1993.

Douglas, Nigel. *Legendary Voices*. London: Andre Deutsch, Limited, 1992.

Dramer, Dan. *Monsters: 21 Stories of the Most Fantastic and Gruesome Creatures of All Time*. Providence, RI: Jamestown Publishers, 1985.

Durell, Ann, and Marilyn Sachs, editors. *The Big Book of Peace*. New York: Dutton Children's Books, 1990.

Edwards, Judith. *Lewis and Clark's Journey of Discovery in American History*. Springfield, NJ: Enslow Publications, Inc., 1999.

Epstein, Lawrence J. *A Treasury of Jewish Anecdotes*. Northvale, NJ: Jason Aronson, Inc., 1989.

Fecher, Msgr. Vincent. *"The Lord and I": Vignettes from the Life of a Parish Priest*. New York: Alba House, 1990.

Feinberg, David B. *Queer and Loathing: Rants and Raves of a Raging AIDS Clone*. New York: Viking, 1994.

Feinstein, Stephen. *The 1950s: From the Korean War to Elvis*. Berkeley Heights, NJ: Enslow Publications, Inc., 2000.

Finley, Carol. *The Art of African Masks*. Minneapolis, MN: Lerner Publications Company, 1999.

Fletcher, Lynne Yamaguchi. *The First Gay Pope and Other Records*. Boston, MA: Alyson Publications, Inc., 1992.

Flynn, Tom, and Karen Lound. *AIDS: Examining the Crisis*. Minneapolis, MN: Lerner Publications Company, 1995.

Ford, Michael Thomas. *It's Not Mean If It's True*. Los Angeles, CA: Alyson Books, 2000.

Ford, Michael Thomas. *The Voices of AIDS: Twelve Unforgettable People Talk About How AIDS has Changed Their Lives*. New York: Morrow Junior Books, 1995.

Fradin, Dennis Brindell. *Lincoln's Birthday*. Hillside, NJ: Enslow Publications, Inc., 1990.

Fradin, Dennis Brindell. *Patrick Henry: "Give Me Liberty or Give Me Death!"* Hillside, NJ: Enslow Publications, Inc., 1990.

Freeman, Dorothy Rhodes. *St. Patrick's Day*. Berkeley Heights, NJ: Enslow Publications, Inc., 1992.

Frist, Karyn McLaughlin, editor. *"Love you, Daddy Boy": Daughters Honor the Fathers They Love*. Lanham, MD: Taylor Trade Publishing, 2006.

Galas, Judith C. *Gay Rights*. San Diego, CA: Lucent Books, 1996.

Garvey, Rev. Francis J. *Favorite Humor of Famous Americans*. Kandiyohi, MN: Rev. Francis J. Garvey, 1981.

Glenn, Menahem G. *Israel Salanter: Religious-Ethical Thinker*. New York: Bloch Publishing Company, 1953.

Goldenstern, Joyce. *American Women Against Violence*. Springfield, NJ: Enslow Publications, Inc., 1998.

Goldstein, Ernest. *The Statue* Abraham Lincoln: *A Masterpiece by Daniel Chester French*. Minneapolis, MN: Lerner Publications Company, 1997.

Goldwasser, Rabbi Dovid. *It Happened in Heaven: Personal Stories of Inspiration*. Jerusalem: Feldheim Publishers, 1995.

Gow, Mary. *Robert Hooke: Creative Genius, Scientist, Inventor*. Berkeley Heights, NJ: Enslow Publishers, Inc., 2006.

Green, Carl R., and William R. Sanford. *Judge Roy Bean*. Springfield, NJ: Enslow Publications, Inc., 1995.

Greenberg, Jan, and Sandra Jordan. *Andy Warhol: Prince of Pop*. New York: Delacorte Press, 2004.

Greenberg, Keith Elliot. *An Armenian Family*. Minneapolis, MN: Lerner Publications Company, 1997.

Greenfeld, Howard. *Marc Chagall*. New York: Harry N. Abrams, Inc., 1990.

Gregory, Dick. *Nigger: An Autobiography*. With Robert Lipsyte. New York: Dutton, 1964.

Guernsey, JoAnn Bren. *Voices of Feminism: Past, Present, and Future*. Minneapolis, MN: Lerner Publications Company, 1996.

Haney, Lynn. *Ride 'em, Cowgirl!* New York: G.P. Putnam's Sons, 1975.

Harmon, Ron L. *American Civil Rights Leaders*. Berkeley Heights, NJ: Enslow Publications, Inc., 2000.

Himelstein, Shmuel. *Words of Wisdom, Words of Wit*. Brooklyn, NY: Mesorah Publications, Ltd., 1993.

Hunter, Sally M. *Four Seasons of Corn: A Winnebago Tradition*. Minneapolis, MN: Lerner Publications Company, 1997.

Jenkins, Ron. *Acrobats of the Soul*. New York: Theatre Communications Group, Inc., 1988.

Jillette, Penn. *God, No! Signs You May Already be an Atheist and Other Magical Tales*. New York: Simon and Schuster, 2011.

Johnson, Harry "Steamboat." *Standing the Gaff: The Life and Hard Times of a Minor League Umpire*. Introduction to the Bison Book edition by Larry R. Gerlach. Lincoln, NE: University of Nebraska Press, 1994.

Jones, Betty Millsaps. *Wonder Women of Sports*. New York: Random House, 1981.

Jones, Tim. *Dog Heroes*. Fairbanks, AK: Epicenter Press, 1995.

Josephson, Judith Pinkerton. *Allan Pinkerton: The Original Private Eye*. Minneapolis, MN: Lerner Publications Company, 1996.

Kallen, Stuart A. *Great Composers*. San Diego, CA: Lucent Books, 2000.

Karsh, Yousuf. *Canadians*. Toronto: University of Toronto Press, 1978.

Karsh, Yousuf. *Karsh: A Biography in Images*. Boston, MA: MFA Publications, 2003.

Knapp, Ron. *American Legends of Rock*. Springfield, NJ: Enslow Publications, Inc., 1996.

Krull, Kathleen. *Lives of the Artists: Masterpieces, Messes (and What the Neighbors Thought)*. San Diego, CA: Harcourt Brace & Company, 1995.

Lang, Paul. *Maria Tallchief: Native American Ballerina*. Springfield, NJ: Enslow Publications, Inc., 1997.

Lasky, Kathryn. *A Brilliant Streak: The Making of Mark Twain*. San Diego, CA: Harcourt Brace and Company, 1998.

Lassieur, Allison. *Leonardo da Vinci and the Renaissance in World History*. Berkeley Heights, NJ: Enslow Publications, Inc., 2000.

Lawton, Mary. *Schumann-Heink: The Last of the Titans*. New York: The Macmillan Company, 1928.

Lazo, Caroline. *Alice Walker: Freedom Writer*. Minneapolis, MN: Lerner Publications Company, 2000.

Lehn, Cornelia. *Peace Be with You*. Newton, KS: Faith and Life Press, 1980.

Leipold, L. Edmond. *Famous American Artists*. Minneapolis, MN: T.S. Denison and Company, Inc., 1969.

Lemke, Nancy. *Missions of the Southern Coast*. Minneapolis, MN: Lerner Publications Company, 1996.

Lester, Julius. *The Blues Singers: Ten Who Rocked the World*. New York: Hyperion Books for Children, 2001.

Levine, Ellen. *Anna Pavlova: Genius of the Dance*. New York: Scholastic, Inc., 1995.

Levine, Ellen. *Freedom's Children: Young Civil Rights Activists Tell Their Own Stories*. New York: G.P. Putnam's Sons, 1993.

Lipman, Steve. *Laughter in Hell: The Use of Humor during the Holocaust*. Northvale, NJ: Jason Aronson, Inc., 1991.

MacMillan, Dianne M. *Martin Luther King, Jr. Day*. Hillside, NJ: Enslow Publications, Inc., 1992.

Macnow, Glen. *Sports Great Tiger Woods*. Berkeley Heights, NJ: Enslow Publishers, Inc., 2001.

Marston, Elsa. *Muhammad of Mecca: Prophet of Islam*. New York: Franklin Watts, 2001.

McCormick, Anita Louise. *Native Americans and the Reservation in American History*. Springfield, NJ: Enslow Publications, Inc., 1996.

McPhee, Nancy. *The Book of Insults*. New York: St. Martin's Press, 1978.

Menard, Valerie, and Sue Boulais. *Trent Dimas*. Childs, MD: Mitchell Lane Publishers, Inc., 1998.

Mercredi, Morningstar. *Fort Chipewyan Homecoming: A Journey to Native Canada*. Minneapolis, MN: Lerner Publications Company, 1997.

Metil, Luana, and Jace Townsend. *The Story of Karate: From Buddhism to Bruce Lee*. Minneapolis, MN: Lerner Publications Company, 1995.

Meyer, Susan E. *Mary Cassatt*. New York: Harry N. Abrams, Inc., 1990.

Mingo, Jack. *The Juicy Parts*. New York: The Berkley Publishing Group, 1996.

Moore, Michael. *Downsize This!* New York: HarperPerennial, 1997.

Moore, Michael. *Stupid White Men*. New York: HarperCollins Publishers, Inc., 2001.

Mosher, Bill. *Visionaries*. Maryknoll, NY: Orbis Books, 1995.

Nardo, Don. *Philip II and Alexander the Great Unify Greece in World History*. Berkeley Heights, NJ: Enslow Publications, Inc., 2000.

Nardo, Don. *Rulers of Ancient Rome*. San Diego, CA: Lucent Books, 1999.

Nichols, Richard. *A Story To Tell: Traditions of a Tlingit Community*. Minneapolis, MN: Lerner Publications Company, 1998.

O'Brien, Steven. *Antonio López de Santa Anna*. New York: Chelsea House Publishers, 1992.

O'Brien, Steven. *Pancho Villa*. New York: Chelsea House Publishers, 1994.

Old, Wendie. *Marian Wright Edelman: Fighting for Children's Rights.* Springfield, NJ: Enslow Publications, Inc., 1995.

Oleksy, Walter. *Christopher Reeve.* San Diego, CA: Lucent Books, 2000.

Oliver, Marilyn Tower. *Gay and Lesbian Rights: A Struggle.* Springfield, NJ: Enslow Publications, Inc., 1998.

Orleans, Ellen. *Can't Keep a Straight Face.* Bala Cynwyd, PA: Laugh Lines Press, 1992.

Orleans, Ellen. *Still Can't Keep a Straight Face.* Bala Cynwyd, PA: Laugh Lines Press, 1996.

Osho. *Osho on Zen: A Stream of Consciousness Reader.* Los Angeles, CA: Renaissance Books, 2001.

Patner, Andrew. *I.F. Stone: A Portrait.* New York: Doubleday, 1988.

Peters, Russell M. *Clambake: A Wampanoag Tradition.* Minneapolis, MN: Lerner Publications Company, 1992.

Pettit, Jayne. *A Place to Hide: True Stories of Holocaust Rescues.* New York: Scholastic, Inc., 1993.

Pflueger, Lynda. *Thomas Nast: Political Cartoonist.* Berkeley Heights, NJ: Enslow Publications, Inc., 2000.

Pinsky, Mark I. *The Gospel According to The Simpsons.* Louisville, KY: Westminster John Knox Press, 2001.

Primack, Ben, adapter and editor. *The Ben Hecht Show: Impolitic Observations from the Freest Thinker of 1950s Television.* Jefferson, NC: McFarland & Company, Inc., Publishers, 1993.

Ramone, Dee Dee. *Poison Heart: Surviving the Ramones.* With Veronica Kofman. Wembley, Middlesex, England: Firefly Publishing, 1997.

Rawding, F.W. *Gandhi and the Struggle for India's Independence.* Minneapolis, MN: Lerner Publications Company, 1982.

Reed, Jennifer. *Leonardo da Vinci: Genius of Art and Science.* Berkeley Heights, NJ: Enslow Publishers, Inc., 2005.

Reef, Catherine. *Paul Laurence Dunbar: Portrait of a Poet.* Berkeley Heights, NJ: Enslow Publications, Inc., 2000.

Regguinti, Gordon. *The Sacred Harvest: Ojibway Wild Rice Gathering.* Minneapolis, MN: Lerner Publications Company, 1992.

Rench, Janice E. *Understanding Sexual Identity: A Book for Gay Teens and Their Friends.* Minneapolis, MN: Lerner Publications Company, 1990.

Reynolds, Moira Davison. *Women Champions of Human Rights.* Jefferson, NC: McFarland and Company, Inc., 1991.

Rodriguez, Consuelo. *Cesar Chavez.* New York: Chelsea House Publishers, 1991.

Roessel, Monty. *Kinaaldá: A Navajo Girl Grows Up*. Minneapolis, MN: Lerner Publications Company, 1993.

Rogers, Fred. *You Are Special*. New York: Viking, 1994.

Sanford, Herb. *Ladies and Gentlemen, The Garry Moore Show: Behind the Scenes When TV was New*. New York: Stein and Day, Publishers, 1976.

Savage, Jeff. *Gold Miners of the Old West*. Springfield, NJ: Enslow Publications, Inc., 1995.

Schraff, Anne. *Coretta Scott King: Striving for Civil Rights*. Springfield, NJ: Enslow Publications, Inc., 1997.

Schuman, Michael A. *Martin Luther King: Leader for Civil Rights*. Springfield, NJ: Enslow Publications, Inc., 1996.

Schwager, Tina, and Michele Schuerger. *Gutsy Girls: Young Women Who Dare*. New York: Scholastic, Inc., 1999.

Sheafer, Silvia Anne. *Women in America's Wars*. Springfield, NJ: Enslow Publications, Inc., 1996.

Shephard, Marie Tennent. *Maria Montessori: Teacher of Teachers*. Minneapolis, MN: Lerner Publications Company, 1996.

Sherrow, Victoria. *The Oklahoma City Bombing*. Springfield, NJ: Enslow Publications, Inc., 1998.

Shields, Charles J. *I am Scout: The Biography of Harper Lee*. New York: Henry Holt and Company, 2008.

Shindler, Phyllis, collector. *Raise Your Glasses*. London: Judy Piatkus, Limited, 1988.

Shore, Nancy. *Amelia Earhart*. New York: Chelsea House Publishers, 1987.

Smaridge, Norah. *Hands of Mercy: The Story of Sister-Nurses in the Civil War*. New York: Benziger Brothers, Inc., 1960.

Spies, Karen Bornemann. *Franklin Delano Roosevelt*. Springfield, NJ: Enslow Publications, Inc., 1999.

Stewart, Whitney. *The 14th Dalai Lama: Spiritual Leader of Tibet*. Minneapolis, MN: Lerner Publications Company, 1996.

Strickland, Michael R. *African-American Poets*. Springfield, NJ: Enslow Publications, Inc., 1996.

Telushkin, Rabbi Joseph. *Jewish Wisdom: Ethical, Spiritual, and Historical Lessons from the Great Works and Thinkers*. New York: William Morrow and Company, Inc., 1994.

Waldron, Ann. *Francisco Goya*. New York: Harry N. Abrams, Inc., 1992.

Warren, Roz, editor. *Women's Glibber: State-of-the-Art Women's Humor*. Freedom, CA: The Crossing Press, 1992.

Wilson, Suzan. *Stephen King: King of Thrillers and Horror*. Berkeley Heights, NJ: Enslow Publications, Inc., 2000.

Woog, Adam. *Bill Gates*. San Diego, CA: Lucent Books, 1999.

Wukovits, John F. *Colin Powell*. San Diego, CA: Lucent Books, 2000.

Wukovits, John F. *George W. Bush*. San Diego, CA: Lucent Books, 2000.

Yamane, Linda. *Weaving a California Tradition: A Native American Basketmaker*. Minneapolis, MN: Lerner Publications Company, 1997.

Youngman, Henny. *Take My Life, Please!* With Neal Karlen. New York: William Morris and Company, Inc., 1991.

Yount, Lisa. *William Harvey: Discoverer of How Blood Circulates*. Hillside, NJ: Enslow Publishers, Inc., 1994.

Appendix B: About the Author

It was a dark and stormy night. Suddenly a cry rang out, and on a hot summer night in 1954, Josephine, wife of Carl Bruce, gave birth to a boy — me. Unfortunately, this young married couple allowed Reuben Saturday, Josephine's brother, to name their first-born. Reuben, aka "The Joker," decided that Bruce was a nice name, so he decided to name me Bruce Bruce. I have gone by my middle name — David — ever since.

Being named Bruce David Bruce hasn't been all bad. Bank tellers remember me very quickly, so I don't often have to show an ID. It can be fun in charades, also. When I was a counselor as a teenager at Camp Echoing Hills in Warsaw, Ohio, a fellow counselor gave the signs for "sounds like" and "two words," then she pointed to a bruise on her leg twice. Bruise Bruise? Oh yeah, Bruce Bruce is the answer!

Uncle Reuben, by the way, gave me a haircut when I was in kindergarten. He cut my hair short and shaved a small bald spot on the back of my head. My mother wouldn't let me go to school until the bald spot grew out again.

Of all my brothers and sisters (six in all), I am the only transplant to Athens, Ohio. I was born in Newark, Ohio, and have lived all around Southeastern Ohio. However, I moved to Athens to go to Ohio University and have never left.

At Ohio U, I never could make up my mind whether to major in English or Philosophy, so I got a bachelor's degree with a double major in both areas, then I added a Master of Arts degree in English and a Master of Arts degree in Philosophy. Yes, I have my MAMA degree.

Currently, and for a long time to come (I eat fruits and veggies), I am spending my retirement writing books such as *Nadia Comaneci: Perfect 10*, *The Funniest People in Comedy*, *Homer's* Iliad: *A Retelling in Prose*, and *William Shakespeare's* Hamlet: *A Retelling in Prose*.

If all goes well, I will publish one or two books a year for the rest of my life. (On the other hand, a good way to make God laugh is to tell Her your plans.)

By the way, my sister Brenda Kennedy writes romances such as *A New Beginning* and *Shattered Dreams*.

Appendix C: Some Books by David Bruce

Anecdote Collections

250 Anecdotes About Opera
250 Anecdotes About Religion
250 Anecdotes About Religion: Volume 2
250 Music Anecdotes
Be a Work of Art: 250 Anecdotes and Stories
The Coolest People in Art: 250 Anecdotes
The Coolest People in the Arts: 250 Anecdotes
The Coolest People in Books: 250 Anecdotes
The Coolest People in Comedy: 250 Anecdotes
Create, Then Take a Break: 250 Anecdotes
Don't Fear the Reaper: 250 Anecdotes
The Funniest People in Art: 250 Anecdotes
The Funniest People in Books: 250 Anecdotes
The Funniest People in Books, Volume 2: 250 Anecdotes
The Funniest People in Books, Volume 3: 250 Anecdotes
The Funniest People in Comedy: 250 Anecdotes
The Funniest People in Dance: 250 Anecdotes
The Funniest People in Families: 250 Anecdotes
The Funniest People in Families, Volume 2: 250 Anecdotes
The Funniest People in Families, Volume 3: 250 Anecdotes
The Funniest People in Families, Volume 4: 250 Anecdotes
The Funniest People in Families, Volume 5: 250 Anecdotes
The Funniest People in Families, Volume 6: 250 Anecdotes
The Funniest People in Movies: 250 Anecdotes
The Funniest People in Music: 250 Anecdotes
The Funniest People in Music, Volume 2: 250 Anecdotes
The Funniest People in Music, Volume 3: 250 Anecdotes
The Funniest People in Neighborhoods: 250 Anecdotes
The Funniest People in Relationships: 250 Anecdotes
The Funniest People in Sports: 250 Anecdotes
The Funniest People in Sports, Volume 2: 250 Anecdotes
The Funniest People in Television and Radio: 250 Anecdotes
The Funniest People in Theater: 250 Anecdotes

The Funniest People Who Live Life: 250 Anecdotes
The Funniest People Who Live Life, Volume 2: 250 Anecdotes
The Kindest People Who Do Good Deeds, Volume 1: 250 Anecdotes
The Kindest People Who Do Good Deeds, Volume 2: 250 Anecdotes
Maximum Cool: 250 Anecdotes
The Most Interesting People in Movies: 250 Anecdotes
The Most Interesting People in Politics and History: 250 Anecdotes
The Most Interesting People in Politics and History, Volume 2: 250 Anecdotes
The Most Interesting People in Politics and History, Volume 3: 250 Anecdotes
The Most Interesting People in Religion: 250 Anecdotes
The Most Interesting People in Sports: 250 Anecdotes
The Most Interesting People Who Live Life: 250 Anecdotes
The Most Interesting People Who Live Life, Volume 2: 250 Anecdotes
Reality is Fabulous: 250 Anecdotes and Stories
Resist Psychic Death: 250 Anecdotes
Seize the Day: 250 Anecdotes and Stories

---

[1] Source: Carlos Sadovi, Tara Malone and Lisa Black, "Chicago public school students skip class in show of activism." *Chicago Tribune*. 3 September 2008 <http://www.chicagotribune.com/news/local/ chi-boycott_03sep03,0,7085986.story>. Also: Paul Tough, "Free the Chicago 1,400[1]." Slate.com. 9 September 2008 <http://www.slate.com/blogs/blogs/ schoolhouse/default.aspx>.

[2] Source: Dianne M. MacMillan, *Martin Luther King, Jr. Day*, pp. 5, 26, 38-39.

[3] Source: Andrew Sullivan, "Princeton's Proposition 8." *The Daily Dish*. 21 November 2008 <http://andrewsullivan.theatlantic.com/the_daily_dish/2008/11/ princetons-prop.html>.

[4] Source: Ron L. Harmon, *American Civil Rights Leaders*, pp. 88, 90.

[5] Source: Michael Thomas Ford, *The Voices of AIDS*, pp. 207-208.

[6] Source: Amita Parashar, "Queen Margaret." *The Advocate*. 10 July 2009 <http://www.advocate.com/exclusive_detail_ektid96524.asp>.

[7] Source: Tom Flynn and Karen Lound, *AIDS: Examining the Crisis*, pp. 47, 49.

[8] Source: Karen Alonso, Loving v. Virginia: *Interracial Marriage*, p. 40.

[9] Source: Kae Cheatham, *Dennis Banks: Native American Activist*, pp. 24-25.

---

1. http://www.slate.com/blogs/blogs/schoolhouse/archive/2008/09/09/free-the-chicago-1-400.aspx

[10]Source: Anne Schraff, *Coretta Scott King: Striving for Civil Rights*, p. 53.

[11] Source: Walter Oleksy, *Christopher Reeve*, pp. 57-58.

[12]Source: Joyce Goldenstern, *American Women Against Violence*, p. 30.

[13] Source: Bryan Appleyard, "Ice queen Catherine Deneuve remembers." *The Times*. 18 January 2009 <http://entertainment.timesonline.co.uk/tol/arts_and_entertainment/film/article5523771.ece>.

[14]Source: David B. Feinberg, *Queer and Loathing: Rants and Raves of a Raging AIDS Clone*, pp. 47-48.

[15] Source: Glen Macnow, *Sports Great Tiger Woods*, pp. 14-16, 41-42, 48-49.

[16]Source: Ellen Levine, *Anna Pavlova: Genius of the Dance*, p. 94.

[17]Source: Tom Flynn and Karen Lound, *AIDS: Examining the Crisis*, pp. 15, 30. 34, 58-59.

[18]Source: Michael Thomas Ford, *The Voices of AIDS*, pp. 66-67.

[19]Source: Toller Cranston, *Zero Tollerance*, p. 314.

[20]Source: David B. Feinberg, *Queer and Loathing: Rants and Raves of a Raging AIDS Clone*, p. 183.

[21]Source: Ron Chernow, *The Death of the Banker*, pp. 11-12.

[22]Source: Jack Mingo, *The Juicy Parts*, p. 123.

[23] Source: Tim Jones, *Dog Heroes*, pp. 34-35.

[24] Source: Osho, *Osho on Zen: A Stream of Consciousness Reader*, p. 17.

[25]Source: Dan Dramer, *Monsters*, p. 38.

[26]Source: Ernest Goldstein, *The Statue* Abraham Lincoln: *A Masterpiece by Daniel Chester French*, pp. 26-27.

[27]Source: Allison Lassieur, *Leonardo da Vinci and the Renaissance in World History*, p. 114.

[28]Source: Carol Finley, *The Art of African Masks*, pp. 14, 38.

[29] Source: Yousuf Karsh, *Karsh: A Biography in Images*, p. 126.

[30]Source: Susan E. Meyer, *Mary Cassatt*, p. 81.

[31]Source: Linda Yamane, *Weaving a California Tradition: A Native American Basketmaker*, pp. 15, 17.

[32] Source: Kathryn Lasky, *A Brilliant Streak: The Making of Mark Twain*, p. 10.

[33]Source: Don Nardo, *Philip II and Alexander the Great Unify Greece in World History*, p. 44.

[34] Source: John F. Wukovits, *George W. Bush*, p. 19.

[35]Source: Stephen Feinstein, *The 1950s: From the Korean War to Elvis*, p. 53.

[36] Source: Adam Woog, *Bill Gates*, p. 64.

[37]Source: Mary Lawton, *Schumann-Heink: The Last of the Titans*, pp. 79-80.

[38]Source: Catherine Corley Anderson, *Jackie Kennedy Onassis: Woman of Courage*, pp. 62, 65-66, 85-86.

[39]Source: Ben Primack, adapter and editor, *The Ben Hecht Show*, pp. 166-167.

[40] Source: Mary Gow, *Robert Hooke: Creative Genius, Scientist, Inventor*, pp. 64-66.

[41]Source: Richard Nichols, *A Story To Tell: Traditions of a Tlingit Community*, pp. 30-31.

[42]Source: Harry "Steamboat" Johnson, *Standing the Gaff*, p. xiii.

[43]Source: Nancy Lemke, *Missions of the Southern Coast*, p. 25.

[44] Source: Simon Doonan, *Nasty*, pp. 252-253.

[45] Source: Consuelo Rodriguez, *Cesar Chavez*, pp. 54-55.

[46]Source: F.W. Rawding, *Gandhi and the Struggle for India's Independence*, p. 47. Also: Menahem G. Glenn, *Israel Salanter: Religious-Ethical Thinker*, p. 106. Also: "Upcoming Auction Of Gandhi's Belongings Creates Fallout." NPR. 26 February 2009. < https://www.npr.org/templates/story/story.php?storyId=101182076# >.

[47]Source: Dennis Brindell Fradin, *Lincoln's Birthday*, pp. 35-36.

[48]Source: Catherine Corley Anderson, *Jackie Kennedy Onassis: Woman of Courage*, pp. 63-64.

[49] Source: Steve O'Brien, *Pancho Villa*, pp. 100-101.

[50]Source: Ann Waldron, *Francisco Goya*, p. 78.

[51]Source: Nigel Douglas, *Legendary Voices*, p. 68.

[52]Source: Fred Rogers, *You Are Special*, p. 17.

[53] Source: Jennifer Reed, *Leonardo da Vinci: Genius of Art and Science*, pp. 41, 43.

[54]Source: Dennis Brindell Fradin, *Lincoln's Birthday*, p. 8

[55]Source: Don Nardo, *Rulers of Ancient Rome*, p. 76.

[56]Source: Howard Greenfeld, *Marc Chagall*, p. 83.

[57]Source: A. Monroe Aurand, Jr., *Wit and Humor of the Pennsylvania Germans*, p. 12.

[58]Source: Lynn Haney, *Ride 'em, Cowgirl!*, p. 51.

[59]Source: Marie Tennent Shephard, *Maria Montessori: Teacher of Teachers*, pp. 15, 18-19, 28.

[60]Source: Jan Greenberg and Sandra Jordan, *Andy Warhol: Prince of Pop*, pp. 100-102.

[61] Source: Ellen Levine, *Freedom's Children: Young Civil Rights Activists Tell Their Own Stories*, p. 34.

[62]Source: Susan Banfield, *Ethnic Conflicts in School*, pp. 22-24, 28-29.

[63]Source: Maggi Aitkens, *Kerry, a Teenage Mother*, pp. 27-28.

[64]Source: Nancy Shore, *Amelia Earhart*, pp. 26-27.

[65]Source: Michael Moore, *Stupid White Men*, p. 115.

[66] Source: Charles J. Shields, *I am Scout: The Biography of Harper Lee*, pp. 71-72.

[67] Source: Malcolm Glad, "The Uses of Adversity." *The New Yorker*. 10 November 2008 <http://www.newyorker.com/reporting/2008/11/10/081110fa_fact_gladwell?currentPage=all>.

[68] Source: S. Claus, *Holiday Cheer for the 19th Hole*, p. 74.

[69]Source: Wendie Old, *Marian Wright Edelman: Fighting for Children's Rights*, p. 14.

[70]Source: Linda Yamane, *Weaving a California Tradition: A Native American Basketmaker*, p. 18.

[71] Source: Osho, *Osho on Zen: A Stream of Consciousness Reader*, pp. 96-97.

[72]Source: Luana Metil and Jace Townsend, *The Story of Karate: From Buddhism to Bruce Lee*, p. 75.

[73]Source: Lynda Pflueger, *Thomas Nast: Political Cartoonist*, p. 49.

[74]Source: Rev. Francis J. Garvey, *Favorite Humor of Famous Americans*, p. 15.

[75]Source: Michael Thomas Ford, *It's Not Mean If It's True*, p. 190.

[76]Source: Toller Cranston, *Zero Tollerance*, p. 250.

[77]Source: Michael D. Cole, *The Titanic: Disaster at Sea*, pp. 26, 36-37.

[78] Source: Steven O'Brien, *Antonio López de Santa Anna*, pp. 78-79.

[79] Source: Roger Ebert, "Campaigning with Paul Newman." *Chicago Sun-Times*. 30 September 2008 <http://rogerebert.suntimes.com/apps/pbcs.dll/article?AID=/20080930/PEOPLE/809309997>.

[80] Source: Karyn McLaughlin Frist, editor, *"Love you, Daddy Boy": Daughters Honor the Fathers They Love*, p. 25.

[81] Source: Andrew Patner, *I.F. Stone: A Portrait*, p. 118.

[82] Source: Nancy Lemke, *Missions of the Southern Coast*, pp. 30-33.

[83] Source: Gordon Regguinti, *The Sacred Harvest: Ojibway Wild Rice Gathering*, p. 17.

[84] Source: Wayne Dosick, *The Business Bible*, pp. 173-174.

[85] Source: Feodor Ivanovitch Chaliapine, *Pages From My Life: An Autobiography*, p. 127. Also: Kathleen Krull, *Lives of the Artists*, p. 27.

[86] Source: Sally M. Hunter, *Four Seasons of Corn: A Winnebago Tradition*, p. 15. Also: Harry Thomas, a Winnebago Native American.

[87] Source: Michael A. Schuman, *Martin Luther King: Leader for Civil Rights*, p. 21.

[88] Source: Herb Sanford, *Ladies and Gentlemen, The Garry Moore Show: Behind the Scenes When TV was New*, p. 79. Also: Jessica R. Glass, et al. "Was Frozen Mammoth or Giant Ground Sloth Served for Dinner at The Explorers Club?" PLoS One.[2] 2016; 11(2): e0146825. Published online 2016 Feb 3. doi: 10.1371/journal.pone.0146825[3]. https://www.ncbi.nlm.nih.gov/pmc/articles/PMC4740485/

[89] Source: Elsa Marston, *Muhammad of Mecca: Prophet of Islam*, p. 43.

[90] Source: Richard Nichols, *A Story To Tell: Traditions of a Tlingit Community*, p. 40.

[91] Source: Penn Jillette, *God, No! Signs You May Already be an Atheist and Other Magical Tales*, pp. 62-63.

[92] Source: Moira Davison Reynolds, *Women Champions of Human Rights*, p. 13.

[93] Source: Ron Knapp, *American Legends of Rock*, p. 59.

---

2. https://www.ncbi.nlm.nih.gov/pmc/articles/PMC4740485/

3. https://doi.org/10.1371%2Fjournal.pone.0146825

[94]Source: Stuart A. Kallen, *Great Composers*, p. 101.

[95]Source: Steve Lipman, *Laughter in Hell*, p. 113.

[96] Source: Deb Price, "Schools Get Timely, Gay-Friendly Reminders." Creators.com. 11 August 2008 <http://www.creators.com/opinion/deb-price/schools-get-timely-gay-friendly-reminders.html>. Also: "Anti-Gay School Earns A Hard Slapdown[4]." 15 May 2008 <http://bluecollarscientist.com/tag/ponce-de-leon-high-school/>.

[97]Source: Judith C. Galas, *Gay Rights*, pp. 19-20, 22.

[98]Source: Janice E. Rench, *Understanding Sexual Identity: A Book for Gay Teens and Their Friends*, pp. 9-10.

[99]Source: Chastity Bono, *Family Outing*, p. 214.

[100]Source: Lynne Yamaguchi Fletcher, *The First Gay Pope and Other Records*, p. 72.

[101] Source: John F. Wukovits, *Colin Powell*, pp. 87-89.

[102]Source: Ellen Levine, *Anna Pavlova: Genius of the Dance*, p. 106.

[103] Source: Jayne Pettit, *A Place to Hide: True Stories of Holocaust Rescues*, pp. 99-101.

[104]Source: Shmuel Himelstein, *Words of Wisdom, Words of Wit*, p. 88.

[105] Source: Norah Smaridge, *Hands of Mercy: The Story of Sister-Nurses in the Civil War*, p. 66.

[106]Source: Dan Dramer, *Monsters*, pp. 54-56.

[107]Source: JoAnn Bren Guernsey, *Voices of Feminism: Past, Present, and Future*, p. 60.

[108]Source: Gay Block and Malka Drucker, *Rescuers: Portraits of Moral Courage in the Holocaust*, pp. 197-198, 200-201.

[109] Source: Jayne Pettit, *A Place to Hide: True Stories of Holocaust Rescues*, pp. 100-103.

[110] Source: Nick Del Calzo, creator and photographer, *The Triumphant Spirit*, pp. 98-99.

[111]Source: Gay Block and Malka Drucker, *Rescuers: Portraits of Moral Courage in the Holocaust*, pp. 204, 206.

4.	http://bluecollarscientist.com/2008/05/15/anti-gay-school-earns-a-hard-slapdown/

[112]Source: Chris Crutcher, *King of the Mild Frontier*, pp. 74-75.

[113]Source: Morningstar Mercredi, *Fort Chipewyan Homecoming: A Journey to Native Canada*, p. 18.

[114] Source: Bill Mosher, *Visionaries*, pp. 38-42. 48, 54-56, 63.

[115] Source: Steven O'Brien, *Antonio López de Santa Anna*, pp. 93-94.

[116]Source: Anita Louise McCormick, *Native Americans and the Reservation in American History*, p. 34.

[117]Source: Karen Bornemann Spies, *Franklin Delano Roosevelt*, p. 58.

[118]Source: Ben Primack, adapter and editor, *The Ben Hecht Show*, pp. 77-78.

[119] Source: John Bankston, *Sigmund Freud: Exploring the Mysteries of the Mind*, pp. 28-29.

[120]Source: Silvia Anne Sheafer, *Women in America's Wars*, pp. 79, 86.

[121]Source: Carl R. Green and William R. Sanford, *Judge Roy Bean*, pp. 32-33.

[122] Source: Karyn McLaughlin Frist, editor, *"Love you, Daddy Boy": Daughters Honor the Fathers They Love*, p. 34.

[123]Source: Msgr. Vincent Fecher, *"The Lord and I": Vignettes from the Life of a Parish Priest*, p. 40.

[124]Source: Nancy McPhee, *The Book of Insults*, pp. 126, 151.

[125]Source: Dick Gregory, *Nigger*, Dedication.

[126]Source: Ellen Orleans, *Can't Keep a Straight Face*, pp. 32-34.

[127] Source: Mary Gow, *Robert Hooke: Creative Genius, Scientist, Inventor*, pp. 5-6.

[128]Source: Lynda Pflueger, *Thomas Nast: Political Cartoonist*, p. 108.

[129] Source: Tom Danehy, "The city doesn't need nice leadership; it needs tough, smart, focused leadership." *Tucson Weekly*. 30 April 2009 <http://www.tucsonweekly.com/tucson/danehy/Content?category=1063741>.

[130]Source: Roxane Chadwick, *Anne Morrow Lindbergh: Pilot and Poet*, p. 42.

[131]Source: Michael Thomas Ford, *It's Not Mean If It's True*, p. 120.

[132]Source: Suzan Wilson, *Stephen King: King of Thrillers and Horror*, p. 108.

[133]Source: Carl R. Green and William R. Sanford, *Judge Roy Bean*, p. 20.

[134] Source: Glenn Garvin, "Larry King dishes lots of dirt in new autobiography." McClatchy Newspapers. 17 July 2009

<http://www.popmatters.com/pm/article/108387-larry-king-dishes-lots-of-dirt-in-new-autobiography/>.

[135] Source: Simon Doonan, *Nasty*, pp. 1, 97.

[136] Source: W.K. Breckenridge, *Anecdotes of Great Musicians*, p. 31.

[137] Source: Jack Mingo, *The Juicy Parts*, pp. 214-215.

[138] Source: Neil Steinberg, "Luminary for the little man." *Chicago Sun-Times.* 1 November 2008 <http://www.suntimes.com/news/metro/1253521,studs-terkel-dies-103108.article>.

[139] Source: L. Edmond Leipold, *Famous American Artists*, pp. 30-32.

[140] Source: Rabbi Dovid Goldwasser, *It Happened in Heaven*, p. 53.

[141] Source: Adam Woog, *Bill Gates*, p. 51.

[142] Source: Jerry Clower, *Stories from Home*, p. 40.

[143] Source: Shmuel Himelstein, *Words of Wisdom, Words of Wit*, p. 89.

[144] Source: Ron Jenkins, *Acrobats of the Soul*, p. 128.

[145] Source: Nigel Douglas, *Legendary Voices*, p. 43.

[146] Source: Willis Barnstone, translator, *Greek Lyric Poetry*, p. 134.

[147] Source: Moira Davison Reynolds, *Women Champions of Human Rights*, p. 56.

[148] Source: Rabbi Joseph Telushkin, *Jewish Wisdom*, p. 579.

[149] Source: Consuelo Rodriguez, *Cesar Chavez*, pp. 24-25.

[150] Source: Andrea Broadwater, *Marian Anderson: Singer and Humanitarian*, pp. 59- 65, 100, 114.

[151] Source: Mary Lawton, *Schumann-Heink: The Last of the Titans*, p. 287.

[152] Source: W.K. Breckenridge, *Anecdotes of Great Musicians*, p. 43.

[153] Source: Michael Moore, *Stupid White Men*, p. 61.

[154] Source: Yousuf Karsh, *Karsh: A Biography in Images*, p. 179.

[155] Source: Lynne Yamaguchi Fletcher, *The First Gay Pope and Other Records*, p. 106. Also: "America the Beautiful." Wikipedia. Accessed 11 September 2023. < https://en.wikipedia.org/wiki/America_the_Beautiful >.

[156] Source: Lawrence J. Epstein, *A Treasury of Jewish Anecdotes*, pp. 8-9.

[157]Source: Janice E. Rench, *Understanding Sexual Identity: A Book for Gay Teens and Their Friends*, pp. 16-17.

[158]Source: Jeff Savage, *Gold Miners of the Old West*, pp. 18, 20.

[159]Source: Andrew Patner, *I.F. Stone: A Portrait*, pp. 13, 126.

[160]Source: Paul Lang, *Maria Tallchief: Native American Ballerina*, pp. 86-87.

[161]Source: Dennis Brindell Fradin, *Patrick Henry: "Give Me Liberty or Give Me Death!"*, pp. 33, 35.

[162]Source: Whitney Stewart, *The 14th Dalai Lama: Spiritual Leader of Tibet*, pp. 24, 49.

[163]Source: F.W. Rawding, *Gandhi and the Struggle for India's Independence*, pp. 5, 27.

[164]Source: Michael R. Strickland, *African-American Poets*, pp. 47, 67.

[165]Source: Paul Lang, *Maria Tallchief: Native American Ballerina*, pp. 49-50.

[166] Source: John F. Wukovits, *George W. Bush*, pp. 27-28.

[167]Source: Judith Pinkerton Josephson, *Allan Pinkerton: The Original Private Eye*, pp. 90, 92.

[168]Source: Russell M. Peters, *Clambake: A Wampanoag Tradition*, pp. 21, 25-26.

[169]Source: Monty Roessel, *Kinaaldá: A Navajo Girl Grows Up*, pp. 10, 19. Also: "Navaho Nation." Wikipedia. Accessed 13 November 2023. < https://en.wikipedia.org/wiki/Navajo_Nation >.

[170]Source: Gordon Regguinti, *The Sacred Harvest: Ojibway Wild Rice Gathering*, p. 15.

[171]Source: Anita Louise McCormick, *Native Americans and the Reservation in American History*, pp. 59-60.

[172] Source: Ann Durell and Marilyn Sachs, editors, *The Big Book of Peace*, pp. 39-45. Also: Cornelia Lehn, *Peace Be with You.*, pp. 65-66. In this second book, the name is spelled Seth Loflin.

[173] Source: Nick Del Calzo, creator and photographer, *The Triumphant Spirit*, pp. 30-31.

[174]Source: Dorothy Rhodes Freeman, *St. Patrick's Day*, p. 42. Also: "Irish flag." Wikipedia. Accessed 13 September 2023. < https://en.wikipedia.org/wiki/ Flag_of_Ireland >.

[175]Source: Tina Schwager and Michele Schuerger, *Gutsy Girls*, p. 36.

[176]Source: Regina Barreca, editor, *New Perspectives on Women and Comedy*, p. 19.

[177] Source: Lisa Yount, *William Harvey: Discoverer of How Blood Circulates*, pp. 61, 63.

[178]Source: JoAnn Bren Guernsey, *Voices of Feminism: Past, Present, and Future*, p. 23.

[179]Source: Michael Moore, *Downsize This!*, pp. 236ff, 311.

[180]Source: Nancy Shore, *Amelia Earhart*, pp. 17-18.

[181]Source: Roz Warren, editor, *Women's Glibber*, p. 119.

[182]Source: Rabbi Joseph Telushkin, *Jewish Wisdom*, p. 124.

[183]Source: Mark I. Pinsky, *The Gospel According to The Simpsons*, p. 5.

[184]Source: Rev. Francis J. Garvey, *Favorite Humor of Famous Americans*, pp. 15-16.

[185]Source: Lawrence J. Epstein, *A Treasury of Jewish Anecdotes*, pp. 120-121.

[186] Source: Helen Thomas, "Palin + McCain Equals More Bush." Commondreams.org. 19 September 2008 <http://www.commondreams.org/view/2008/09/19-7>.

[187]Source: Dianne M. MacMillan, *Martin Luther King, Jr. Day*, pp. 10-11, 21-22.

[188]Source: Wendie Old, *Marian Wright Edelman: Fighting for Children's Rights*, pp. 21-22.

[189]Source: Bob Bernotas, *Spike Lee: Filmmaker*, p. 76.

[190]Source: Victoria Sherrow, *The Oklahoma City Bombing*, pp. 25, 39.

[191]Source: Susan Banfield, *Ethnic Conflicts in School*, p. 26.

[192]Source: Ron L. Harmon, *American Civil Rights Leaders*, p. 47.

[193] Source: Bill Deane, *Bob Gibson*, p. 17.

[194]Source: Andrea Broadwater, *Marian Anderson: Singer and Humanitarian*, p. 73. Marilyn Tower Oliver, *Gay and Lesbian Rights: A Struggle*, pp. 52-53.

[195] Source: Penn Jillette, *God, No! Signs You May Already be an Atheist and Other Magical Tales*, pp. 43-47.

[196]

[197]Source: Caroline Lazo, *Alice Walker: Freedom Writer*, pp. 34-45.

[198]Source: Alexander Cho, "Passion Play." 30 October 2005 <http://www.frontierspublishing.com/features/feature_second.html>.

[199]Source: Michael A. Schuman, *Martin Luther King: Leader for Civil Rights*, pp. 17-18.

[200]Source: Anne Schraff, *Coretta Scott King: Striving for Civil Rights*, pp. 16-17.

[201]Source: Keith Elliot Greenberg, *An Armenian Family*, p. 24.

[202]Source: Paul Bailey, editor, *The Stately Homo: A Celebration of the Life of Quentin Crisp*, p. 159.

[203]Source: Bob Dole, *Great Presidential Wit*, p. 37.

[204]Source: Bob Dole, *Great Presidential Wit*, p. 95.

[205] Source: Roger Ebert, "The third most important story of the year." Blogs.suntimes.com. 13 November 2008 <http://blogs.suntimes.com/ebert/2008/11/the_third_most_important_story.html#more>.

[206]Source: Whitney Stewart, T*he 14th Dalai Lama: Spiritual Leader of Tibet*, pp. 66, 68.

[207]Source: Michael Boo, *The Story of Figure Skating*, pp. 32-34.

[208]Source: Kae Cheatham, *Dennis Banks: Native American Activist*, pp. 22-23.

[209] Source: Jonah Lehrer, "Daydream achiever." *Boston Globe*. 31 August 2008 <http://www.boston.com/bostonglobe/ideas/articles/2008/08/31/daydream_achiever/?page=full>.

[210]Source: Keith Elliot Greenberg, *An Armenian Family*, p. 33.

[211]Source: Judith Edwards, *Lewis and Clark's Journey of Discovery in American History*, pp. 24, 64, 67.

[212]Source: Stuart A. Kallen, *Great Composers*, p. 41.

[213]Source: L. Edmond Leipold, *Famous American Artists*, p. 76.

[214]Source: Joyce Goldenstern, *American Women Against Violence*, p. 92.

[215] Source: Luana Metil and Jace Townsend, *The Story of Karate: From Buddhism to Bruce Lee*, p. 55.

[216]Source: Steve Lipman, *Laughter in Hell*, p, 196.

[217] Source: S. Claus, *Holiday Cheer for the 19th Hole*, p. 81.

[218] Source: A. Monroe Aurand, Jr., *Wit and Humor of the Pennsylvania Germans*, p. 8.

[219] Source: Elsa Marston, *Muhammad of Mecca: Prophet of Islam*, p. 79.

[220] Source: Dennis Brindell Fradin, *Patrick Henry: "Give Me Liberty or Give Me Death!"*, pp. 21, 23.

[221] Source: Bob Dole, *Great Political Wit*, pp. 8, 15, 23-24.

[222] Source: Karen Bornemann Spies, *Franklin Delano Roosevelt*, pp. 39-40.

[223] Source: Phyllis Shindler, collector, *Raise Your Glasses*, p. 21.

[224] Source: Charles J. Shields, *I am Scout: The Biography of Harper Lee*, p. 99.

[225] Source: Caroline Lazo, *Alice Walker: Freedom Writer*, pp. 20-21.

[226] Source: Yousuf Karsh, *Canadians*, pp. 98-99.

[227] Source: Mary L. Davis, *Women Who Changed History: Five Famous Queens of Europe*, pp. 56-57.

[228] Source: Yousuf Karsh, *Canadians*, pp. 76-77.

[229] Source: Dorothy Rhodes Freeman, *St. Patrick's Day*, p. 37.

[230] Source: Ernest Goldstein, *The Statue* Abraham Lincoln: *A Masterpiece by Daniel Chester French*, pp. 32, 34-35.

[231] Source: Kathryn Lasky, *A Brilliant Streak: The Making of Mark Twain*, p. 19.

[232] Source: Catherine Reef, *Paul Laurence Dunbar: Portrait of a Poet*, pp. 29-30.

[233] Source: Betty Millsaps Jones, *Wonder Women of Sports*, pp. 14-18.

[234] Source: Valerie Menard and Sue Boulais, *Trent Dimas*, pp. 7, 20-23, 27-28.

[235] Source: Tina Schwager and Michele Schuerger, *Gutsy Girls*, pp. 116-117.

[236] Source: Herb Sanford, *Ladies and Gentlemen, The Garry Moore Show: Behind the Scenes When TV was New*, pp. 140-141.

[237] Source: Tim Jones, *Dog Heroes*, p. 35.

[238] Source: Norah Smaridge, *Hands of Mercy: The Story of Sister-Nurses in the Civil War*, pp. 19-20.

[239] Source: Dee Dee Ramone, *Poison Heart: Surviving the Ramones*, pp. 14-15.

[240] Source: Don Nardo, *Rulers of Ancient Rome* pp. 28-29.

[241] Source: Jerry Clower, *Stories from Home*, p. 134.

[242] Source: Don Nardo, *Philip II and Alexander the Great Unify Greece in World History*, p. 73.

[243] Source: John F. Wukovits, *Colin Powell*, p. 67.

[244] Source: Phyllis Shindler, collector, *Raise Your Glasses*, p. 116.

[245] Source: Allison Lassieur, *Leonardo da Vinci and the Renaissance in World History*, pp. 18-19.

[246] Source: Julius Lester, *The Blues Singers: Ten Who Rocked the World*, p. 37.

[247] Source: Malcolm Glad, "The Uses of Adversity." *The New Yorker*. 10 November 2008 <http://www.newyorker.com/reporting/2008/11/10/081110fa_fact_gladwell?currentPage=all>.

[248] Source: Steve O'Brien, *Pancho Villa*, pp. 25-26.

[249] Source: Jeff Savage, *Gold Miners of the Old West*, pp. 34-35.

[250] Source: Judith Pinkerton Josephson, *Allan Pinkerton: The Original Private Eye*, pp. 35-36, 48-49, 76, 103ff.

[251] Source: Ellen Levine, *Freedom's Children: Young Civil Rights Activists Tell Their Own Stories*, p. 136.

[252] Source: Henny Youngman, *Take My Life, Please!*, p. 89.

[253] Source: Silvia Anne Sheafer, *Women in America's Wars*, pp. 49-50.